Meditations for the Newly Married

Meditations
for the
Newly
Married

Third Edition

John M. Drescher

HERALD PRESS
Scottdale, Pennsylvania
Waterloo, Ontario

Library of Congress Cataloging-in-Publication Data
Drescher, John M.
     Meditations for the newly married / by John M. Drescher. — 3rd ed.
          p.   cm.
     Includes bibliographical references.
     ISBN 0-8361-9017-3 (alk. paper)
     1. Married people—Prayer-books and devotions—English.
     I. Title.
     BV4596.M3D7 1995
     242'.64—dc20   95-1292
                                                                          CIP

The paper used in this publication is recycled and meets the minimum require-
ments of American National Standard for Information Sciences Permanence of
Paper for Printed Library Materials, ANSI Z39.48-1984.

Except as otherwise noted, the Bible text is from *The New Revised Standard Version
Bible,* copyright 1989, by the Division of Christian Education of the National
Council of the Churches of Christ in the USA, and is used by permission.

MEDITATIONS FOR THE NEWLY MARRIED
Copyright ©1969, 1986, 1995 by Herald Press, Scottdale, PA 15683
     Published simultaneously in Canada by Herald Press,
     Waterloo, Ont N2L 6H7. All rights reserved
Library of Congress Catalog Number: 95-1292
International Standard Book Number: 0-8361-9017-3
Printed in the United States of America
Cover and design by Julie Kauffman

00 99 98 97 96 95   19 18 17 16 15 14 13
87,500 copies in print

To my loving wife
BETTY
God's gift to me

Contents

3. Devoted to Worthy Objectives

Preface

These meditations, woven from the threads of scriptural teaching and human experience, speak to the marriage relationship.

Today more than ever, many people are urging a return to the spiritual springs of marriage. May such springs be discovered here.

Both the rigors and the romance of the marriage relationship are referred to in these meditations. May those who read receive the strength that will sustain them through the difficult days and may such also receive the kind of insight which will spur them on to a more mature and enlarging love.

I see my audience as the newly married with perhaps a sprinkling of couples who hope to be married soon. Perchance also some who have been married for years will find help from these pages.

All who enter marriage have dreams. These meditations were written with the desire that they may help in finding the fulfillment of these dreams and the realization of the great realities God has reserved for those who enter marriage.

This small volume is the result of jottings and ideas gathered over the years from many books, articles, and talks on marriage and the home. I have also had the privilege of counseling couples before and after marriage, as well as teaching numerous courses on the Christian family. It is impossible for me to give the sources and references for all the ideas and thoughts shared here. Where I am able I have attempted to do so.

Because some who read these pages may desire to read further on these and other subjects, I include a short list of books in the back. It is also a good practice for husband and wife to take time to read together at least one good book each year on the marriage relationship.

My prayer is that the messages from the Scriptures, the meditations, beautitudes, and prayers shared here will inspire not only in the early days of marriage but in the years ahead.

1

Developed After the Divine Pattern

Blessed is that marriage
In which each receives the other
As a gift from God
To love and cherish.

Such shall know
A deepening devotion and desire
For each other,
And both will know God
Daily a little better.

The Lord God said, "It is not good for the man to be alone.
I will make a helper suitable for him." . . . Then the Lord
God made a woman . . . and he brought her to the man.
—Genesis 2:18, 22, NIV

Gifts from God

Read Genesis 2:18-24

When the world was in its freshness of new beauty and its beginning, God placed the first family in the purity of that primal paradise. After giving the bride away, God personally performed the marriage ceremony and pronounced a blessing. Woman is God's gift to man. Man is God's gift to woman.

Every marriage is like the dawn of a new day. It is ushered in with joy and anticipation and perhaps some fear. Will marriage be all that you hoped for? Will love remain as large as it seemed at the altar? Will your loved one always be as beautiful as at the beginning? These questions hover over every new home.

This is your day. You anticipated it. You planned for it. Every true friend wishes you well.

And now your wedding ceremony is over. Your married life has begun. Almost like magic and in a matter of minutes, everything changes. You now live together in the intimacies of an entirely new life.

In a sense, your previous relationship was artificial. Until now you met under favorable circumstances. You were prepared for each other. Now life cannot be artificial. It is lived too close. You will be together always—when circumstances are favorable and unfavorable; when you are prepared and unprepared; when you are rested and fatigued; in sunshine and struggle, delight and disappointment. You will no longer see, feel, act, understand, or pray the same. Yours is now a shared life.

Your heart tells you that you dare let nothing enter to mar the happiness of your relationships. Marriage is a multiplier. It makes life twice as satisfying, if you will bend every effort to make it so. It is true also that marriage can multiply sorrow, heartache, and suffering if lovers become lax in their efforts to make each other happy.

To share at the deepest levels of life does not happen automatically. It takes planning, purpose, and constant watchfulness. Do not hesitate to always give your best.

Now life calls you to a quest;
To laugh, to love, to work, to play,
To serve, to sacrifice, to pray.
Life calls—give it your best.
        —Author Unknown

For all this you will need humility, honesty, and mutual helpfulness. You will be sustained by the shared strength and the combined comfort of one another and of God.

At your wedding you were reminded that marriage is a glorious provision of God: "Dearly beloved, we are gathered together here in the sight of God, and in the face of this company, to join together this man and this woman in holy matrimony, which is an honorable estate instituted by God." Each wedding is a reminder that the loving hand of our heavenly Father withholds no good thing from you. He places you also by marriage in a paradise of possibilities. These possibilities present themselves to you today and always.

But you were not left at the marriage altar. Nor does God leave you there. In one sense you set sail upon an uncharted sea. Yet it is not uncharted. There are maps. Stars still shine. Heaven and earth are interested in helping. And God promises to give guidance.

> *The voice that breathed o'er Eden,*
> *That earliest wedding day,*
> *The primal marriage blessing,*
> *It hath not passed away.* —John Keble

PRAYER

Dear Father, may every dawn bring a new burst of gratitude for my beloved, Your gift to me. May every noontime bring a serene awareness of my beloved's support. May every evening bring the joy of continued oneness and every day's ending bring a deepening knowledge and peace that you have made us for each other. What you have joined together let no one put asunder. Amen.

It is a fusion of two hearts—the union of two lives—the coming together of two tributaries, which after being joined in marriage will flow in the same channel, in the same direction . . . carrying the same burdens of responsibility and obligation.

—Peter Marshall, quoted by Catherine Marshall in her book A Man Called Peter, 1951

From this hour the summer rose
   Sweeter breathes to charm us;
From this hour the winter snows
   Lighter fall to harm us:
Fair or foul—on land or sea—
   Come the wind or weather,
Best and worst, whate'er they be,
   We shall share together.
     —Winthrop Mackworth Praed

They are no longer two, but one flesh.—Matthew 19:6

The Miracle of Marriage

Read Mark 10:6-9

isten to an ancient legend: "Originally man and woman were one. However, in the course of history, they were somehow separated, cut in half. From that time to this, each one is seeking the lost part in order to be united again."

An old rabbinic writing says it this way: "The man is restless while he misses the rib that was taken from his side, and the woman is restless until she gets under the man's arm, from whence she came."

The ancient myth and rabbinic saying are profoundly true. Some may smile at the story of how woman was made from man's rib. Yet, to say the least, it is a great symbol of the way husband and wife are to regard each other.

When two people marry, they become one—but which one? The answer is neither one. Marriage blends and binds the two together. Each becomes what the other is.

Marriage is a mathematical miracle. In it, one plus one does not equal two. God says that if you take one woman and add one man, you still have one.

As marriage partners, you are joined in such an intimate

and real way that you can be called "one flesh." This extremely strong language God uses to describe the marriage union means that no part of the husband's or wife's personality remains unaffected after marriage. There is to be a mysterious and magnificent blending of body and spirit. No other earthly relationship is as close or has as much power to enable and exalt.

Even the child which remains for a short time in the warmth and wonder of the mother's womb is finally separated forever to become distinctly different. But from the moment of marriage, husband and wife move to become one.

This oneness does not mean that God designed husband and wife to be identical. In the literal sense, God's creation of a "helpmeet" means "a completing, a counterpart, one suitable to." The marriage partner is one who helps to fill the empty places of the other.

This does not mean always seeing blissfully eye to eye. You can't be completed with what you already have. If there is one thing more beautiful than the beginning of a marriage, it is when that beginning is lost in a growing oneness of soul and spirit.

There is victory and growing in completeness and togetherness when husband and wife become more of themselves because of the other—when there is a complementing of each other rather than a competition with each other.

Yes, in a real sense, you are no longer two but one. Never again do you need to face life alone. Every thought and act can be shared with one who loves you and knows you better than any other. Sorrow, sickness, failure, success, and ambitions need not be kept to oneself. Whatever happens in failure or fortune, you have each other to depend upon.

In marriage you surrender the privilege of a private life. Marriage is the unveiling of hearts and bodies to each other. It is an act of trust and acceptance in every respect. Otherwise the full meaning of marriage cannot be realized.

From now on you belong to each other. You accept each other as you accept yourself. Privacy and pretense are put away.

When, in your embrace, you gaze into each other's eyes, you are saying, "You are mine, all mine," and "I am yours, all yours."

PRAYER

O God, our Father, we cannot see tomorrow, but we can trust your leading. We cannot comprehend the mystery of marriage, but we can come to you for greater knowledge. We cannot hope for every day to be easy, but we can come asking for enablement for whatever arises. For these privileges we offer our praise. Amen.

Blessed is that marriage
Which learns early;
Fear hardens the heart
While love unlocks
And softens it.

Such shall be lighted
By the lamp of love,
Dispelling darkness
And giving gladness
In the presence of gloom.

Such shall know love
Which drives out despair
By the tender touch
Of encouragement.

What God has joined together, let no one separate.
—Mark 10:9

Love
Is for Life

Read Matthew 19:4-9 and Romans 7:2

o anyone who reads the New Testament, there can be no doubt that marriage is a lifelong commitment. Those who take their marriage vows seriously and really look to God for happiness and guidance consider that they are married for life. They will not walk out on each other. Anything which undermines such thinking regarding marriage is sinful.

A wise man wrote words which every married couple should consider carefully: "The massed experience of mankind would justify us in saying to any young couple who sets out on the career of love, 'Now hold together. Hold together even when the light seems to have gone out, and your way looks dark and dull. Hold together even though it hurts.' "

We don't give up the ship because of an occasional storm. Well-adjusted couples will recognize moments of rapture and moments of disappointment because marriage is filled with both hopes and hazards. When we think of it, a diamond is nothing but a piece of coal that stuck together at the same spot for years and years under terrific pressure. A happy marriage is not a marriage with the least trouble but a marriage in which each partner has learned to practice love when pressure is on.

Just because the going gets difficult at times does not mean a marriage is doomed. Sometimes young people in the haze of romance and glamour think that the first quarrel has ruined their marriage. On the contrary, it may mark the beginning of a unity achieved by toil and tears and talking together.

Regardless of what moderns may think, the Scriptures clearly state that marriage is to be permanent. The enduring reality of the marriage union is so strongly expressed and dignified by God that it is compared to the union which exists between Christ and his church.

The wedding vows include the promise to love, to honor, to cherish until death parts. We enter marriage persuaded of its permanence. Without this, small difficulties will easily drive apart. To enter marriage with the idea of dissolving it if it doesn't work out, cripples marriage at its beginning.

What greater thing is there for two human souls
Than to feel that they are joined for life—
To strengthen each other in all labor.
To rest on each other in all sorrow,
To minister to each other in all pain,
To be one with each other in silent unspeakable memories
At the moment of the last parting.—George Eliot

The divine blueprint for marriage is clear. Whether we will be able to build according to that blueprint depends on us and our relationship to God, the Great Architect.

Likely it is true as someone suggested, "There never was a marriage which could not have failed, and there never was a marriage which could not have succeeded." The elements of disharmony are always present in a home. But to those whose love for God and for one another remains strong, no sickness can weaken love's hold, no ill fortune can shake love's foundation, hard times cannot snuff out love's spirit, and no separation can diminish its noble steadfastness and unwavering loyalty.

PRAYER

O God, we thank you that you are more interested in our possibilities than in our past failures. Take away the shadows of the soul which seem to lodge there because of faults and failings of the past. Deliver us from needless apprehension or fear of the future. Give such brightness of soul which doesn't change with the weather and such serenity of soul which is not shaken by storm. In Christ call us to such cheerfulness and good courage so that we may lift each other to love life and win the battle. Amen.

Six things are requisite to create a "happy home." Integrity must be the architect, and tidiness the upholsterer. It must be warmed with affection, lighted up with cheerfulness; and industry must be the ventilation, renewing the atmosphere and bringing in fresh salubrity day by day; while over all, as a protecting canopy and glory, nothing will suffice except the blessing of God.—James Hamilton

My dearest, when I love God more, I love you the way you ought to be loved.—George McDonald, to his wife

*Husbands, in the same way, show consideration for your
wives in your life together . . . so that nothing may hinder
your prayers. Finally, all of you, have unity of spirit, sympathy, love for one another, a tender heart, and a humble
mind.—1 Peter 3:7-8*

Husbands,
Love Your Wives

group of schoolchildren were asked, "Who is
boss at your house?" The overwhelming majori-
ty reported Mother was. A sprinkling said Father
was. One boy was not sure. "I don't know who is boss at our
house," he wrote. "They are still arguing about it."

St. Paul was probably not a married man, but he gave some
sound advice on the love a husband should have for his wife.
In one paragraph (Ephesians 5:25-31) he gives profound direc-
tions to husbands. He refers not to a "lord relationship" but to
a "love relationship."

1. Love to the point of self-sacrifice. "Husbands, love your
wives, just as Christ loved the church and gave himself up for
her." This speaks of a serving, giving, unselfish, and sacrificial
love. No work is too hard, no sacrifice is too great, no involve-
ment is too demanding for the man who loves and is loved. At
the death of a certain wife, one person suggested that perhaps
God's judgment was upon the husband because he loved his
wife too much. "Impossible," said another. "Can we measure
the love of Christ for his church?" A husband's principal need
tends to be recognition, while a wife's primary need is typical-

ly affection. And a husband proves his love by forgetting himself out of devotion to his wife.

2. Love to the point of purifying the life. "Love your wives, just as Christ loved the church . . . to make her holy by cleansing her with the washing of water by the word, so as to present the church to himself in splendor, without a spot or wrinkle . . . so that she may be holy and without blemish."

A husband brings out the best in his wife in improved physical, emotional, intellectual, and spiritual health when his wife is assured he loves her and she accepts fully the love of her husband. If a wife is beautiful at forty, her husband bears some responsibility for it. Love purifies and beautifies.

A wife's first basic need is to be loved and have that love expressed. Seldom will any husband have reason to doubt his wife's affection for him if he continually gives her assurance by word and action that she is the most important and loved person in his life. "And he praises her" is a phrase from Proverbs. A wife blossoms under the warmth of her husband's praise.

3. Love to the point of positive care and concern. "Husbands should love their wives as they do their own bodies. He who loves his wife loves himself. For no one ever hates his own body, but he nourishes and tenderly cares for it, just as Christ does for the church."

Another basic need for the wife is to sense security. And she finds such security in a husband who has a deep, growing love based on mutual respect and understanding. The husband is to care for his wife as he cares for his own body.

Love does not desire to dominate. Love asks to love. The husband's strength is his wife's protection. His character is her boast and pride. His heart is her haven. As a husband receives a radiance and sense of responsibility in a wife's sensitivity and helpfulness, so a wife grows secure in the shadows of a husband's strength and sympathy.

4. Love to the point of detachment from parents. "Therefore a man leaves his father and his mother and clings to his wife, and they become one flesh." A husband proves his love for his wife by his willingness to separate himself emotionally and in

every other way from his parents. Apron strings must be cut if the home is to be happy. First loyalty and love is now to his wife. Thus another basic need of the wife, that of domestic fulfillment, is met. The wife now has a husband who she knows is all hers and who provides a place which is distinctly her own.

PRAYER

Dear Lord, make us fit to live with. Keep us from taking ourselves too seriously. When we lack patience and gentleness, help us to seek forgiveness and to forgive. Keep us kind. Help us not to harbor hostilities in our hearts toward any. Teach us this, not only once but daily. Amen.

Blessed is that wife
Whose thoughts for her husband
Drive out self-pity
And make him her chief joy.

Blessed is that husband
Whose love for his wife
Keeps his heart tender
And all his speech kind.

Such shall never lack for music
Or be without a song.
For love's strings shall be in tune,
And the heart will always sing.

A wife should respect her husband.—Ephesians 5:33

Wives, Respect Your Husbands

Read Proverbs 31 and 1 Peter 3:1-6

olomon in Proverbs paints the glowing picture of a marriage relationship in which an industrious, loving wife, who has deep respect for her husband, makes her husband and her home happy. He not only is proud of her; he also praises her. "The heart of her husband doth safely trust in her" (KJV).

John Haywood wrote, "A good wife maketh a good husband." The regard a husband has for his wife flows from the respect the wife has for her husband.

Christian people have always believed that there is a particular pattern of marriage which is pointed to in the Scripture. To follow this pattern promises happiness.

God calls upon the wife to reverence her husband. The word "reverence" derives from a word which means to look at deeply, to see and respect the dignity and place of another. A wife without respect for her husband is like a stove without heat, a lamp without light, a body without life.

Reverence is the result of love (Titus 2:3-4). All true love is grounded in esteem. And the wife inspires the good in her husband by the devotion she shows toward him. Love includes not only the physical but also the daily tender words and acts of kindness. It is made up of trust and confidence. A bit of love is the only "bit" which will bridle the tongue. Respect is revealed by a refusal to hurt the other in any way and a desire to help lift the other higher.

Respect means being subject (Ephesians 5:21-24). "Be subject to one another out of reverence for Christ." The husband, according to Scripture, is the head of the home, and the wife can be the heart of the home only as she honors her husband as the head. Yet headship in the Christian context calls for loving service and leadership, not selfish tyranny. Headship in the home is not a statement referring to superiority but a principle of divine order. When out of order, we do not admire the wife or respect the husband.

Theodore Bovet in *A Handbook to Marriage* writes, "Only an immature wife objects to being 'subordinate' . . . . [She] does not realize that she cannot be fully herself until she is the 'heart' of the association, and that she can only be that when the man is the head. Here again no 'rights' are involved; the question is whether the husband and wife are playing the parts for which they were created in the beginning and which alone can make them happy."

A man stands taller and more tender in the presence of a woman who finds it gratifying and satisfying to be a female. And the Scripture says a wife is at home and happy when she recognizes her husband as head of the home.

Some have said the veil of the bride is a symbol of submission to her bridegroom. At the same time, the term "bridegroom" means "bride's servant." At the old wedding feasts the groom waited upon his bride, to show his willingness to serve her. The American satirist Ambrose Bierce defined marriage as "a community consisting of a master, a mistress, and two slaves, making in all two."

An old preacher once wrote: "A good wife is heaven's last, best gift to a man; his angel of mercy . . . his gem of many virtues, his casket of jewels; her voice his sweetest music; her smiles his brightest day; her kisses the guardian of his innocence; her arms the pale of his safety . . . her industry his surest wealth; her economy his safest steward; her lips his faithful counselors; her bosom the softest pillow of his cares; and her prayers the ablest advocates of heaven's blessings on his head."

There is rich treasure for the woman who will mine the meaning of "let . . . the wife see that she reverence her husband."

PRAYER

O God, thank you that your enabling grace is no less than your calling grace. Make us courageous, for we need courage to share, to bear, to care. Deliver us from discouragement which flows from focusing our minds on the mistakes of others. Turn our eyes to your everlasting love and promises. Amen.

Blessed is that marriage
Where God is partner
In every plan and purpose,
Where love for self
Does not exceed
Love for God and others.

Such shall never walk alone
But find life's pathway
Lined with love returned
And happiness come home.

As for me and my household, we will serve the Lord.
—Joshua 24:15

Marriage Takes a Triangle

Read Joshua 24:15-17

A home built on such a resolution as Joshua made may be shaken by storm, sickness, suffering, unemployment, or death, but it shall not fall. It is founded on a rock. Such a confession is a fortress of Christian faith and the haven of spiritual peace and hope.

When two people share a sense of spiritual commitment and unity, they are starting their marriage with strength and stability. Happy the marriage in which partners pledge together that God shall have his proper place in their home. For marriage takes a triangle with Christ as the head. The closer each comes to Christ, the closer each comes to the other. This holy triangle forms also a cornerstone which holds the entire structure together.

To have Christ in his proper place does not happen automatically even for the best of Christians. It means that husband and wife together, from the first, find ways of acknowledging God in their marriage. This should include a number of things.

First, it should include the cultivation of a personal devotional life. A quiet time of personal Bible reading and prayer will prove of more worth than the greatest wealth.

But beyond the personal devotional life there is the particular privilege to join together in worship. The Scripture, "Where two or three are gathered together in my name, there am I in the midst of them," has special meaning in marriage. God promises his presence in so small a group as is found in every marriage. And there is still tremendous truth in the proverb, "Families that pray together stay together."

The husband and wife who kneel together to sincerely pray will have little difficulty rising together to meet the demands of life. We cannot kneel together before God in prayer and be divided. Thomas Fuller once remarked that prayer should be the "key of the day" and the "lock of the night."

Formed for the purest joys
By one desire possessed,
One aim the zeal of all employ,
To make each other blest.

No bliss can equal theirs
Where such affections meet,
While praise devout, and mingled prayers
Make their communion sweet.—Isaac Watts

In 1 Peter 3:7 the Scripture speaks particularly to husbands. It says the husband is not to be bitter against his wife, lest his prayers be hindered. One of the serious pitfalls to happiness in marriage is an inner bitterness toward each other which often starts with small irritations. If this inner feeling is not confessed and forgiven, prayer life is hindered.

Perhaps right here is one of the greatest hindrances to a happy and holy home. Roots of bitterness, though unseen below the soil, are permitted to grow. Instead of digging them out by confession and forgiveness, they develop until they bear fruit of estrangement and disgust. Roots of bitterness do not disappear themselves. They must be faced frankly and forgiven.

Any ill feeling will frustrate prayer and an interest in the

Bible. It is so easy, especially for the husband, to become inwardly bitter about his wife's actions or desires which seem silly to him. Small irritations grow. "I know," said one husband, "what the Scripture means when it tells husbands to beware of roots of bitterness lest the united prayers of husband and wife and personal prayer life is hindered. The secret to successful prayer and vital Bible study is a humility to confess quickly and sincerely faults and feelings one to another. Here is healing."

Happy the marriage in which partners also pledge to attend church together regularly. If there is to be firm faith, it must include fellowship with the family of God. Here is found mutual encouragement in God.

In the fellowship of God's people there is also a united witness and opportunity to serve. Marriage is not merely living with each other but a joining of hands and hearts with God to serve him and others. Joy comes in joining hands with a person and a cause higher and greater than ourselves.

PRAYER

O God, we thank you for the invitation to cast every care on you. May we never come to the place where we think any care is beneath your concern. Help us not to put prayer off as a last resort while persisting to do all humanly possible first. Help us to keep our relationship with you and with each other in good repair. Amen.

Blessed is that marriage
Where each shares freely
The secret inner self and dreams;
Where love's transparency
Brings hidden hopes and hindrances
Into loving understanding.

Such shall know growth
In being and doing
And self-understanding.
For fears faced freely
Will fade and flee away
In the presence of a larger love.

The man said, "This at last is bone of my bones and flesh of my flesh". . . . And the man and his wife were both naked, and were not ashamed.—Genesis 2:23, 25

The Sanctity of Sex—Attitudes

Read Psalm 37

Often marriages are frustrated by wrong attitudes toward sex. Some individuals have inner feelings or fears that sexual relations are wrong, impure, or less than wholesome. The Scripture says without hesitation that sex is sacred and deliberately created as a part of the divine plan. It is part of that which God called "good." The fact that good things can be abused does not make them shameful or evil when used rightly.

Each husband and wife should be convinced of the rightness, goodness, and blessing of sexual union. Among the first things a married couple must do is come to a deep appreciation of sex. They should speak together freely and frankly until attitudes of hesitancy, fear, shame, or guilt are gone. Otherwise spiritual and physical relationships suffer.

The husband needs to accept his wife fully with all her feminine characteristics. Also the wife needs to accept her husband fully in all his masculine nature. And love is shown by each giving body, mind, and heart without reserve and in complete trust to the other.

A negative attitude to sex will not do. "To be indifferent to the physical expression of love, still more to dislike it, or to feel that it is in some way shameful, is neither superior or virtuous nor refined; it is a symptom of mental illness or maladjustment."

Sex is certainly not the only key to marital happiness, as bread is not the only key to life. But sex is a major key to meaningful marriage. It is a beautiful expression of love and union of personalities. The drive of sexual desire is one of the greatest forces which draw husband and wife together. And it is a normal God-given impulse. Thus also satisfying marital relations have a stabilizing and solidifying effect on marriage.

Sex is not a wrong desire which marriage makes possible to satisfy in secret. It is planned by God for his people to find fulfillment and fruitfulness and in it they are to experience full freedom and joy. Sexual union is meant to produce pleasure, satisfaction, confidence. harmony, self-respect, and growing oneness and love.

A satisfying sexual relationship is an artistic achievement. It is the product of patience, practice, intelligence, and skill. Sexual harmony depends more upon such cultivated virtues as kindness, courtesy, and consideration than upon biological factors.

If the sexual act is approached with the primary thought of what we will get personally, we will actually get very little. Such an attitude can bring disappointment and even disgust instead of gratitude and delight. If our approach is to enrich the other, then each of us will be enriched.

In the sexual union it is especially true that in seeking to meet the other's need our own need is best met. So the secret to sexual harmony is in seeking the happiness of the other.

Jesus placed the stamp of purity on marriage when he said, "Have you not read that the one who made them at the beginning 'made them male and female'. . . ?" So it is that husband and wife should find the desire for sexual union a normal, natural desire for closeness and communion, and an expression of love and affection which has a divine dimension. It is an expression of a divine command to love. It becomes the hallowed declaration of the miracle of marriage oneness.

PRAYER

Our Father, we thank you that you know and care for us completely. Help us to know each other's longings as well as words, intentions as well as acts, hopes as well as failures. May we never become insensitive to sorrow or another's need or narrow our concerns to ourselves alone. Amen.

Blessed is that marriage
Which practices the intimacies of life
Out of love
And does not ask for happiness
So much as the opportunity
To give happiness.

Such shall find deeper joys
Than dreamed possible,
For inhibiting fears
Are removed by love
And latent powers
Unfold and flourish
In love's encouragement.

The husband should give to his wife her conjugal rights, and likewise the wife to her husband. For the wife does not have authority over her own body, but the husband does; likewise the husband does not have authority over his own body, but the wife does. —1 Corinthians 7:3-4

The Sanctity of Sex—Actions

ot only is there need for correct perception regarding sex, but there also must be some clarity regarding the practice of sexual relations in marriage. Sometimes couples read a book or two on sexual techniques, then find out that their experience does not correspond. They become discouraged or disillusioned and think their experience is unique.

While books can be of great help, it remains true that there just is no one right way. Each husband and wife need to seek for that which is most satisfying to both.

Take sexual relations seriously. Invest them with all the warmth and richness possible. Make each experience your deepest expression of mutual love and trust. Remember, a satisfying physical expression can endure only if there is more than the physical present.

Words and actions of love are important at all times. It can be said that sex relations reflect the health of the entire marital relationship even more than they determine it. Practice, giving and receiving, respect, consideration, and devotion build the foundation for a satisfying sex life. And those who do not express love and harmony in other ways seldom, if ever, experience sexual satisfaction.

Further, it is necessary to avoid haste and hurry. It is doubtful if any couple has immediate success. Sometimes it may take months and years. No duet is perfect the first days of practice. But as time passes, each learns the art of yielding and leading to bring out the best potential in the music.

Especially in the early days of marriage, it is good for the husband to remember to be gentle. So also the wife should remember to please her husband and let him know she trusts him completely and gladly accepts him as a man.

First efforts in sexual union are seldom skillful or satisfactory. Anxiety often adds to the difficulty, making it awkward. Yet those who are considerate of each other and who have a sense of humor generally achieve sexual compatibility.

One partner typically will have a stronger sex urge than the other. This is normal. So the Scripture says each should keep the other's need in mind. To neglect the sex side of marriage is dangerous. To ask for continued love and loyalty while withholding this great experience of unity in which love and loyalty of husband and wife is continually renewed is practicing fraud. This can soon develop resentment rather than contentment. The Scripture says, "Do not cheat each other of normal sexual intercourse" (NIV).

Such a discussion raises the question of how often husband and wife engage in sexual union. Studies indicate an average of twice a week with many and wide variations. The important thing is for each husband and wife to be frank and free enough with each other that they reach an experience which pleases both.

Couples who refrain from sexual union too long are likely to become tense and irritable toward each other. Also such open themselves to severe temptations. Those who engage in too frequent intercourse may find the act becoming less meaningful and lose the quality and ideal which it should sustain.

So it is that as life lengthens and love deepens it is reflected in greater joy of physical union. No amount of factual knowledge will help those who do not bring love to the act. When a wife responds passively out of duty, it deprives the act of divine dignity and becomes a drab discharge of obligation. When the husband considers sexual pleasure primarily a personal privilege, the act is robbed of its sublimity and speaks of selfishness and self-centeredness.

But when true love abounds, Charles Hugo Doyle writes, "proper sexual functions in wedlock are the passing from husband to wife of the chalice of love, the wine of which imparts one of the deepest joys man and woman can know on the earth. The wine is of their own vintage and requires expert blending and time to improve its strength and savor" (from *Cana Is Forever*, Doubleday, 1958).

PRAYER

Our Father, today we thank you for creating in us the capacity to love. Forgive our self-centered living. Quicken our love for you and for each other, so that the capacity for compassion, to care and to share, may be increased. May no ill feeling or hate prostitute the precious capacity you have given us to love. Amen.

Blessed is that marriage
Which knows love's climactic reward
In children;
In which the responsibilities and duties
Of parenthood
Are not defined by law
But dictated by love.

Such shall know
An abiding joy
Of family fulfillment
And a devotion
Which is dependable and deep.

God blessed them, and God said to them, "Be fruitful and multiply, and fill the earth. . . ."—Genesis 1:28a

Children are an heritage of the Lord.—Psalm 127:3, KJV

Partners in Procreation

Read Psalm 127 and 128

As God's love overflowed in his creation of man and woman, so the love of husband and wife should overflow into a shared love for children. Marriage normally looks forward to parenthood.

Much in modern life militates against the family. Children do not fit easily into two-career marriages and a concern for fine houses, luxuries, and personal independence. The love and care for children can be overshadowed by a concern for gadgets and things.

Many marriages today suffer from a lack of fulfillment and miss many blessings which build togetherness because the first function of marriage, that of procreation, is put off. Babies are looked upon as burdens rather than blessings. The Scripture "Be fruitful and multiply" calls away from the cult of seeking happiness for only two in marriage.

There is no greater human joy than that of a mother clasping to her breast the child to whom she has given birth. And no man is happier than the father gazing into the eyes of his own infant.

Such joy, of course, is part of God's plan. The child is the product and living bond of parents' love for each other. Children are life's superlative satisfaction.

Children not only bring joy and happiness into the home; they also knit husband and wife more closely together in love and harmony and give new interest and purpose to living.

Some parents are childless as a result of their own selfishness. In other cases God has his own reason for withholding the gift of parenthood. Perhaps that reason is that he wants such to reap the rich rewards of adopting a homeless child.

It is true that children need parents. It is just as true that husband and wife need children.

To stress the importance of parenthood does not say that the size of the family should be determined by unbridled sex indulgence or the lack of planning. Most believe in parenthood but want it to be planned parenthood. The issue is not whether it should be planned or not, but how. This is a matter on which each couple must make a decision—a decision not so much defined by law as dictated by love.

Yes, "children are an heritage of the Lord." Children continually call us above ourselves and make marriage more meaningful and magnificent.

As partners with God, parents fulfill God's plan. In giving children, God honors the home in carrying out his continuing creation and in planning the future. For every parent bears a bond to the past and a responsibility to the future.

Children are God's gift to us. In Scripture children are spoken of as a sure sign of God's blessing upon the marriage. Parents who start and sustain a home and under whose care children grow to be strong and pure, are creators second only to God. Theirs is the precious privilege of being partners with God in procreation.

PRAYER

Our Father, if the blessing of bearing children is ours, give us the deepened devotion which draws us into greater oneness with each other and with you. Help us to see children as gifts from your hand and ourselves as those whom you have allowed to share in the continuance of your creative work. Amen.

Blessed is that marriage
In which each member is ready
to make small sacrifices
With cheerfulness,
In which each turns daily duties
Into love's opportunities.

Such shall dwell
In rich palaces of peace.
They shall see joy and love returned
From unexpected places.

Many waters cannot quench love,
  neither can floods drown it.
If one offered for love all
  the wealth of his house,
it would be utterly scorned.—*Song of Solomon 8:7*

Love That Lasts

Read Galatians 5:22-23

ust as the bridegroom kissed his bride, I saw an old man in the last row lean over and kiss his wife," Roy A. Burkhart writes. "I was so attracted by it I went to them immediately and found that they had been married fifty-two years. They still felt a deep and romantic love, and one could sense a great kinship between them" (from *The Secret of a Happy Marriage*, Harper and Bros., 1949).

The Song of Solomon is a song of a bride and groom who are deeply in love. The Dummelow commentary says, "At the first blush we are surprised to find in the Bible a poem on human love." And the poet Shelley writes, "This song is the only marriage song which can satisfy one truly in love. It establishes the physical aspect of love within the realm of the pure and holy." Every bride and groom should go to the Scriptures and read this love song together.

Solomon says that when love is true it cannot be destroyed by any disaster nor can it be bought with bribes.

A story is told of a farm girl who spoke of sparrows that sang like meadowlarks and of rainbows that formed in the soap bubbles when the dishwater was thrown on the road. Then with bated breath she gave the reason for such fantasy: "My lover kissed my eyes last night."

Marriage means that the one you love has in love chosen you above all others on the earth. And on your wedding day you said:

> "I take thee"—from among all others—
> "to love and cherish"—above all others—
> "till death do us part."

Sir Walter Scott tries to tell what true love is:

> True love's the gift which God has given
> To man alone beneath the heaven;
> It is not fantasy's hot fire
> Whose wishes, soon as granted, fly
> It liveth not in fierce desire—
> With dead desire, it doth not die.
>
> It is the secret sympathy,
> The silver link, the silken tie
> Which heart to heart and mind to mind
> In body and in soul can find.

In Proverbs 30:18-19 we read: "Three things are too wonderful for me; four I do not understand: the way of an eagle in the sky, the way of a snake on a rock, the way of a ship on the high seas, and the way of a man with a girl."

Four things baffled the writer of Proverbs. They are the wonders of nature. The eagle flies with ease through the air leaving no track behind him. The serpent races over the rock without rolling or slipping. A ship plows through the sea following an invisible path and leaving no mark behind. Most wonderful is the relationship of a man with a woman. They meet. Their hearts blend, and their souls are bound together into a lifelong relationship.

The oldest and best-loved stories of history tell us of this love, of the way of a man and woman. And in spite of all our world changes, as it spins in space, couples shall go on loving as their Creator planned.

PRAYER

Our Father, we thank you for the faith you have put in us in trusting us with a home. Continue to weave into the fabric of our faith a free and full commitment to you. When we are distraught in the heat of the day, draw us to yourself so that we might find wholeness. Bring to full fruit in us your own nature of love. Amen.

2

Deepened by Christian Virtues

Love is patient and kind; love is not jealous or boastful; love behaves in a courteous manner, and love thinks of others before thinking of self. It is not irritable, nor does it carry a chip on its shoulder. Love refuses to keep a ledger of injuries or insults received. It does not rejoice in wrong, but glories in the right. Love bears all things, continues to believe the best in everything, and gives power to endure everything. Love never becomes obsolete or comes to an end.—Paraphrase of 1 Corinthians 13:4-8

Your love must be genuine. Hate what is wrong, and hold to what is right. Be affectionate in your love . . . eager to show one another honor. . . .—Romans 12:9-10, Goodspeed

The Meaning of Love

Read 1 Corinthians 13

A movie star is quoted as saying that marriage kills love. She had three marriages which she offered as proof. What a misleading and revealing concept of love!

It is not strange that few encyclopedias carry the word "love." Few have dared to attempt to define love. A complete definition can hardly be given.

Without a doubt the best definition of love is found in 1 Corinthians 13. In these few short sentences love is defined as a far different thing from the love portrayed by the unreal world of entertainment. Love is not mere moonlight, magnolias, or music. True love is defined by what it will do or will not do in relation to others. This is agape love.

Look more closely at these characteristics of love.

Love is *patient*. Love understands and can afford to wait. The one who loves pours the oil of patient love into the machinery of life to lubricate the point of greatest friction. Patient love restrains anger in order to be in a position to help. St. Augustine called patience "the companion of wisdom." Patience plays a particularly important part in handling small annoyances. We can bear the burden of suffering and sickness, but we lose patience when a pencil is misplaced.

Love is *kind*. Kindness is love in fulfilling another's need. Look at each other with the eye of patience. And listen to each other with the ear of kindness. Kindness is love in action. As Joseph Joubert said more than a century ago: "A part of kindness consists in loving people more than they deserve."

Love does *not envy*. Love is glad of its own portion and of another's portion. It does not covet what others have, and it does not begrudge what they have. Love does not detract by act or speech from the stature of another.

Love does *not boast*. Love does not seek to show its own greatness or goodness. It does not play down its faults or brag up its strength. It never speaks about its own success or importance.

Love is *not rude*. Love thinks of others before self. It has an inner thoughtfulness which thinks first of the feelings of others. It is never rude. Nothing of the other's life is inconsequential to love.

Love is *not self-seeking*. It is not cocky about its own position or prominence. Love is ready to give up its rights and even its life for another. For the one who has the capacity to love another is the least concerned about being loved.

Love is *not easily angered*. Love is not touchy or easily ruffled. Love refuses to keep in its memory a record of injuries or insults received. It will not hold a grudge. Shakespeare wrote, "Love is not love which alters when it alternation finds."

Love *keeps no record of wrongs*. It is not suspicious, for suspicion soon smothers a free spirit and saps the very springs of spiritual strength. Suspicion brings only sorrow. Trust builds. The tests of marriage are met by trusting.

Love *rejoices with the truth*. Love cherishes what truth can do. It finds no pleasure in repeating wrong. It looks for opportunities to share the truth.

Love *bears all things* (KJV). It bends beneath the burden of the beloved to bear the other's care. Like a star which lacks luster in the light, love shines best in the dark.

Love *always hopes.* It continues to believe in others when some doubt. It feels for others in their deepest failings and frustrations.

Love *always perseveres.* Love lives by doing and enduring for the sake of others.

Love *never fails.* In every situation seek the way of love. Ask, "How would love act? What would love do?" Love never fails.

PRAYER

Our Father, author of love, we thank you that you have put within us the need for love and the ability to love. Temper all our judgments and thoughts with love and keep our hearts expectant and ready to see love, to receive love, and to give love. Amen.

PRAYER OF FRANCIS OF ASSISI

 Lord, make me an instrument of thy
peace.
Where there is hatred, let me sow love;
Where there is injury, pardon;
Where there is discord, union;
Where there is doubt, faith;
Where there is despair, hope;
Where there is darkness, light;
Where there is sadness, joy;
O Lord, grant that we seek
  Not to be consoled, but to console;
  Not to be understood, but to understand;
  Not to be loved, but to love.
For it is in giving that we receive,
  In forgetting that we find ourselves,
  In pardoning that we are pardoned,
  And in dying that we are born to eternal
    life. Amen.

I am my beloved's,
    and his desire is for me.—Song of Solomon 7:10.

Four Words
for Love

Read Genesis 24

n the Greek language there are four words for love. The first is *eros*. This is a "getting" love. Eros is usually associated with the physical aspect of sexual love. It is the feeling we have when someone pleases, the feeling of desire or sexual passion which responds to lovability. The basic element is desire, a will to possess seeking satisfaction. It sees something desirable in another. It can easily become selfish or shallow, because if the one loved acts or reacts in a manner not desirable, this love grows cold and closes doors of communication and concern.

A second word for love is *stergo*. This is a "caring" love. This is the natural love which we have for others. As human beings we love persons as part of humanity. It is the quiet and abiding feeling within us, which, resting on an object near us, recognizes that we are closely bound together. We are dependent upon each other and obligated to each other. It is the natural love of humans because we sense our oneness with a common humanity. We are concerned about what happens to others because of a common kinship in creation.

Philos is a third word for love. This is a "sharing" love. This word means affection. It is called out of the heart by the pleasure one takes in another. The one loving finds a reflection of his own nature in the person loved. It is based on common interests, common attractions, and close sharing of many things, a sharing which attains its consummation in the sharing of one another's bodies.

A final Greek word for love is *agape,* which is a love called out of one's heart by the preciousness of the one loved. This is a "giving" love. It is a love which impels one to sacrifice for the benefit of the person loved. This love seeks to give rather than to get. Agape love keeps on loving without asking for return.

Now husbands and wives should have all four kinds of love for each other. But unless agape is predominant, unless it controls all the others, the first three will be too empty to endure the difficulties of marriage. Eros, stergo, and philos are not superseded so much by agape as they are controlled and enriched by the agape which permeates every aspect of our relationship.

The love of husband and wife which the Bible speaks of is not eros expressed in sexual passion, or stergo expressed in the obligation to provide for each other, or philos expressed in common interest, but agape which controls all of life so that we seek not our own but the well-being of the other. "I am my beloved's, and his desire is for me" (Song of Solomon 7:10).

Love, as many know it, is simply desire or affection, something which centers in the instincts or the emotions. Christian love has added depths. It comprehends the will as well as emotion, and it looks outward to the beloved rather than inward to its own satisfaction.

So the meaning of love is more than beautiful faces, feelings, figures, or flowers. It is a long day's labor with joy for another. It is spending ourselves until we forget ourselves for another. It is giving ourselves until we forget what is given us. True love does not bargain. It begs to bless.

This kind of love endures through great difficulties because it dies to self in its delight to please the other. Such love is a process of learning and living. It demands a lifetime and will endure a lifetime. In this sense it is as Lamartine wrote, "True love is the ripe fruit of a lifetime" (*Graziella*, part 4, Chapter 3). One of the best definitions of love is that given by one married for many years: "Love is what you've been through with somebody."

> *Yet what is love, good shepherd, sain?*
> *It is a sunshine mixed with rain.*
> —*Sir Walter Raleigh*

PRAYER

Dear Father, as we face the routine responsibilities of married life, grant needed grace for the grind. Free us from the presence of pettiness and pretense. May our love be such that the daily duties shall not be drudgery but acts of devotion and delight. Teach us to tackle the tasks of each day with trust in you and in each other. Amen.

Blessed is that marriage
Which is like a garden
Planted full
Of seeds of joy and love—
At all seasons of the year.

Such shall yield abundant fruit
For every seed will grow
And everyone who sees that garden
Shall of its fullness know.

Love one another . . . outdo one another in showing honor.—Romans 12:10

Love
Is a Plant

Read Ephesians 4:25-32

n fairy tales the story of the beautiful princess and handsome prince ended with the words, "And they lived happily ever after." But in real life a marriage may succeed or fail depending on what is done after wedding.

Marriage is not magic. Neither is the minister a magician. The experience of marriage may pull together or push apart. In a sense a marriage certificate is more of a learner's permit than a guarantee of lifelong happiness.

Love is planted at the beginning of marriage. Now it needs nurture. The mere fact that two persons actually love each other is no guarantee of success. It does not mean that love will grow or remain strong automatically.

Moliere has well said, "Love is the fruit of marriage." And as another writer expressed it, "Marriage is not so much the result of love as the opportunity to love."

Love dare not be taken for granted. It will not coast on momentum. If courtesy, neatness, kindness, and thoughtfulness were fundamental in nurturing love in courtship, then these also are the practices which preserve and deepen love in marriage. Such small things can be spontaneous tributes of love. The absence of these allows a coldness to creep into relationships. Therefore the deference displayed previous to marriage should be sustained after marriage. And such deference demands discipline and decision—the will to love. For the person who says "I can no longer love" has admitted that "I no longer have the will to love."

God meant us for love, but only we can decide whether or not we will be lovable and selfless enough to love in return. No person is free of faults. And the important thing is not that we have faults but what we do with them. It is possible for a husband to see his wife's few faults and be blind to her many strengths. He may complain about her cooking, for example, while all the time he may be blind to the fact that she is a wonderful companion, an efficient housekeeper, and a fine devoted wife.

Then there is that wife who is bothered by her husband who hangs his clothes on the doorknob. This can be aggravating to a neat and tidy wife. Because of one small thing such as this, she may lose sight of the fact that her husband is gentle and kind, ambitious and a good provider.

Love is tested at just such tedious points. And if love is to be nurtured, husband and wife must look for the good. They will also certainly seek to correct annoying habits. For love strives to develop those things which make one lovable. Growth in love will also call us to continue to look for the best in the other and seek excuse for the other's failures.

Love is a plant which dies without constant care. But with careful cultivation it produces fragrant flowers and abundant fruit. True love is not as much feeling as it is faithfulness in carrying out the daily duties promoted by concern for another.

I read one day of a home which was having severe struggles. Tension was building until husband and wife questioned whether real love still existed. One day the wife was suddenly struck with the thought, "Why don't I do the things I know love would dictate, even if I have no particular feeling of love?"

She began, sincerely, in every way possible, to demonstrate

love in the small things of family life. She prepared special dishes in which she knew her husband delighted. She tried to keep her appearance lovable. She asked him about his work. She shared good things which happened during the day and planned her work so that she could relax when her husband was home.

Suddenly both knew something was happening. They doubted their love no longer.

Love is active, not passive. The love that lasts is not so much the love at the marriage altar but the love which grows by carrying out the daily duties of love in the grind of everyday.

Many of today's psychologists believe that feelings follow behavior changes. Feelings do not come first. So the person who says, "I don't feel in love," or "I can no longer love that person," is really saying, "I will not love."

James Russell Lowell described love thus:

It is a thing to walk with, hand in hand,
Through the every-dayness of this workday world.

Shakespeare wrote:

They do not love
That do not show their love.

PRAYER

Our Father, we thank you that your touch can transform. Touch then, we pray, the weaknesses we bring to our marriage and make such show your strength. Touch the strengths we have to share and show how we can better serve you and one another. Touch the love which has led us this far so that it may grow more like yours. Amen.

Blessed is that marriage
In which each partner knows
Love needs nurture
And finds in the small things
Of every day
Opportunity to nourish love
And to continue the ways of courtship.

Such shall know the bliss
Of bringing out the best
In each other
And each shall find
That a word of love
Has greater power
Than the giving of a grand gift.

The Lord appeared to us in the past, saying: "I have loved you with an everlasting love; I have drawn you with loving-kindness."—Jeremiah 31:3, NIV

Love Needs Nurture

William Jennings Bryan was posing for a portrait. The artist asked, "Why do you wear your hair so long?"

"When I was courting Mrs. Bryan, she objected to the way my ears stood out," Bryan replied. "And so to please her I let my hair grow to cover them."

"But that was many years ago," the artist said. "Don't you think you should have your hair cut now?"

"Why," Bryan said with astonishment, "the romance is still going on."

The need for nurturing love never ends. Marriage should be the beginning of romance and not the end of romance. A wife longs to be loved for love's sake. She still seeks to be held daily in her husband's heart and arms, chained by affection. Love grows as one gives witness to it. The reaffirmation "I love you" feeds and strengthens this love.

A husband so easily forgets to speak and share his love. In an interview, one woman expressed her desire: "A caress is better than a career." It is the husband's business to keep that smile on his wife's face and the love-light in her eyes.

A wife must continue to nurture love by such simple things as taking interest in her husband's work and taking time to be with him.

"Most men love their wives only as much as they feel a need to love them, not nearly as much as their wives need loving," W. Clark Ellzey writes in *How to Keep Romance in Your Marriage* (New York: Family Life Library, Association Press). "Most wives encourage their husbands only as much as they feel the need to encourage them, not nearly as much as the average man needs encouragement."

Henry Ward Beecher said it well: "Do not keep the alabaster box of your love and tenderness all sealed up until your friends are all dead. Fill your lives with sweetness. Speak approving, cheery words while their ears can hear them, and while their hearts can be filled with them." This applies especially to husband and wife.

There is of course a sense in which romantic love of early marriage cannot be expected to continue. As love is nurtured, it grows into a deeper love of inward satisfaction and security. The love of the twenties will not do for the thirties. Feelings will be different in the forties. Love is constantly changing. The capacity to love grows from infancy. And the growth of love is limitless.

Love is a thing to be learned. It is built upon the foundation of understanding and common concern. It is cemented together by appreciation and praise. Its construction is maintained and improved by comradeship and continual adjustment. It is beautified by small acts and words of thoughtfulness and kindness.

In addition there are several simple ways to nurture love. First, seek to enjoy each day together. Many persons in planning for the future, forget today. Make it a practice to take time to enjoy each other's presence each day. Remember, now is the time to love. Unless we love now, today, we will never experience love.

Second, develop many mutual interests. The more, the better. The marriage which has the most mutual interests has the most chance of success. A marriage grows as it grows in companionship and comradeship in all its duties and delights.

It is so easy after marriage to become selfish. A husband who would never think of stepping out on his wife for another woman will step out on his wife for nights at the club, sports, and other interests. We nurture love when we plan to do many mutually enjoyable things together. The more life is shared in all its details, the greater is its delight.

Third, develop individual interests which can be shared. A wife by her reading can contribute to the knowledge and interest of her husband. Likewise the husband, through sharing of his everyday contacts, can contribute to his wife's understanding. Such sharing is stimulating and strengthening.

Thus, marriage can become a school of character where love is nurtured by a common sharing in the daily happenings.

PRAYER

Our Father, we thank you that your gifts are the kind that last. Help us in the close tie of marriage to love truth which outlasts time, to seek peace which outlasts adversity, and to radiate a joy which is able to surmount difficult circumstances. Help us never to forget that for love to grow we must mind the small things which nurture love. Amen.

*Blessed is that marriage
In which each keeps
The key of kindness handy
And uses it to open
Every door of discouragement
And loneliness.*

*Such shall unlock the way
Which turns many from wrong
And shall find entrance
To the other's heart.*

Be courteous.—1 Peter 3:8, KJV

Common Courtesy

Read 1 Peter 3:1-12

A newspaper in a large city once estimated that the city's telephone company lost one hundred twenty-five hours a day because its operators used the word "please." Yet the company asked them to use it, believing the gain in goodwill was worth the time spent.

The word "courteous" comes from "kingly"—of the manner of the court. Courteous speech is seasoned with love. It is action motivated by affection.

What many marriages need most is good manners. According to one writer, "Lack of courtesy on the part of a husband or wife, or both, is the basic cause of 80 percent of the coldness and estrangements, if not absolute quarrels and separations, in married life."

Being married does not mean dropping these courtesies practiced before marriage. Rather, they are needed to make the home fragrant. A marriage companion deserves extra courtesy. Someone suggests that the three miracle words in marriage are: "pardon me," "please," and "thank you."

The marriage that has no time for courtesy or compliments will have time for complaints. The marriage that has no time for smiles will have time for frowns, and the marriage that has no time for sweet, loving words will find time for harsh, critical words. We need to decide which kind of marriage we want. We must choose to be courteous and develop the discipline of courtesy from the first day.

I like Henry Drummond's definition of courtesy: "love in little things." Love says "please," because that little word acknowledges the kindness of another person. Love says "thank you," because this expresses gratitude for the other person. Love says "pardon me," because it recognizes the dignity of the other. Love extends small kindnesses and accepts them, because it knows the need for interdependence. Without courtesy love loses its luster and beauty.

Courtesy points to the respect and appreciation we have for each other. Every person wants to be appreciated. Marriage has a way of blossoming when watered with appreciation. And it is not strange that good manners are exercised most in strong and happy homes. Courtesy likely adds years to life.

Courtesy softens and solves misunderstandings. The simple words "I am sorry" or "pardon me" said sincerely have settled many a serious problem. "Anxiety weighs down the human heart, but a good word cheers it up" (Proverbs 12:25). When tempted to speak in haste, remember, "Be courteous."

So also the daily tasks become easy and our work is rewarding by a simple "please" or "thank you" from the lips of one whom we love. As Emerson said, "Life is short, but there is always time for courtesy."

Courtesy and politeness are basic and important means of expressing love. Courtesy avoids words and actions that imply or express disrespect. In many instances the love of husband or wife has been lessened by a scornful, sarcastic, or belittling remark. Critical remarks about one's companion to friends or even to children can cut deeply.

Courtesy does not let one make the other a joke or a laughingstock by relating humorous personal or family incidents before others. Such things cut even though they are meant in good spirit. Wisecracks always weaken a marriage. Teasing is the trademark of hostility. Warm words of love will warm the heart, while careless and complaining words crush the spirit.

Courtesy calls for respect for another's privacy. Such things as refraining from opening the other's mail, staying out of the other's pocketbook, and knocking before opening the bathroom door are simple acts of courtesy which respect the dignity of the other.

No vocation calls for more refinement than marriage. Marriage is no license to descend to a lower level. There is a sense of status and security to a wife whose husband is thoughtful and courteous toward her. Vital to the virtues of womanhood is real respect for her husband, shown in her courteous and polite speech and action toward him.

Remember that manners are more important in marriage than in any other relationship. The wedding day dare never end the day of knighthood or begin the day of serfdom. Courtship must be not only a preparation for marriage but a preservation of marriage. As courtesy was important in courtship, so in marriage manners mirror the soul, revealing attitudes and character and reflecting nobility.

PRAYER

Lord, we thank you because your mercy and love are new every morning. Keep us from being gruff or growly when a favor is asked. Forgive our fretfulness when an opportunity offers itself to help each other. Help us to grow into your likeness—full of love and mercy. Amen.

Blessed is that marriage
In which the members
Avoid the dagger of ill will
And the unkind word
Which stabs the spirit,
As much as they abhor the sword
Which injures the body.

Such shall learn the habit
Of healing hurts
And shall be saved
The sorrow which follows
Hasty words.

Who despises the day of small things?—Zechariah 4:10, NIV

Whoever is faithful in a very little is faithful also in much.—Luke 16:10

Little Things

esterday a great stalwart tree fell to the ground. The day before it stood straight and seemed by all outward appearances strong. The old tree stood as a sapling before America was discovered. Many times lightning had struck it. Storms, earthquakes, and hurricanes had not caused it to fall. Yet tiny beetles began to bore under the tree's bark. They dug into its heart and ate away its mighty fiber. These little insects brought down a giant of the forest. And it is the little things which make or break a marriage.

Separation in most marriages starts and grows because of small irritations. Little things that annoy can become tremendous differences which in time tear two lovers apart. On the other hand, little acts and words of love can create a closeness and charm that is forever cherished and which binds in ever-growing togetherness.

Most of life is made up of little things. But it is the small things that wear the garments of greatness. The small things of life make us glad or sad, lovely or unlovely, considerate or rude. So no one can ignore the little things and grow in love.

Just a touch of the hand, a smile, a careful compliment, a

close caress can work wonders. A little "thank you" has great reward. An offer to help, a small gift selected with care, a favorite flower—these are the stuff of life which builds solid and satisfying marriages. The little words "I love you" and "I'm sorry" enrich, while their absence causes distrust and dullness to creep in.

When a husband and wife drift apart, after one or thirty years, it is because they failed to express love in daily words and acts. Why should little surprises be stopped because we see each other every day? Remember, continuing courtship cultivates an enduring love.

Listen to this interesting story told by one who reminisced about his home: "In my boyhood days my father and mother knew very grave hardship. Yet I recall how whole days of life in our home were glorified and even the hardships seemed light because of my father's graciousness.

"Often early in the morning my father would go out and find the most beautiful rosebud in the rose garden. He would place it at Mother's place to greet her when she came to breakfast. It cost only a few moments of time and a heart full of love. But when he stepped behind her chair as she picked up the rose, and gave her his morning kiss, the whole day was glorified. Even the child who had gotten out of bed 'on the wrong side' and come downstairs in a mood to quarrel felt ashamed because life had been touched by the beauty of love expressed in a small but gracious way."

Many marriages miss meaning then, not because of big things which happen, but because of an overwhelming accumulation of little things. A wife will soon wither like a tender flower if forgotten or taken for granted. A husband will soon grow indifferent if the wife fails to express interest and appreciation in his daily work.

M. A. Kelty wrote, "Small kindnesses, small courtesies, small considerations habitually practiced . . . give a greater charm to the character than the display of great talents and accomplishments."

Of course it must be said that little annoyances, aggravating mannerisms, and thoughtless acts hinder a happy relationship. Beware of the words "You always" or "You never." These carry barbs. And the implications are cutting and unjust.

On the other hand, Julia Carney writes:

Little deeds of kindness, little words of love,
Help to make earth happy like the heaven above.

The smile a wife gives her husband at the end of the day and the kiss and fond word that a husband gives his wife are the small things that bring out the best even in days of darkest disappointment and trial. It is easy to get behind on the small things. But by keeping up on the small things we head off many unnecessary heartaches and know something of heaven right here.

PRAYER

O God, thank you for filling our hearts with high hopes. Help us never to become halfhearted in seeking their fulfillment. Save us from spending our strength in striving for the shallow and superficial. Help us to be faithful in saying and doing the small things which build love and oneness. And lead us so that we may daily learn at least a little more of lasting value. Amen.

Blessed is that marriage
Which makes many friendships
And is devoted to doing good
For God and others.

Such shall see life
Through the wide windows
Of world need,
And from the pleasant porches
Of sacrificial service.

Such shall know
Life is made poor
By keeping,
But made rich
By giving away.

Therefore, be imitators of God, as beloved children, and live in love, as Christ loved us and gave himself up for us.
—Ephesians 5:1-2

I give you a new commandment, that you love one another. Just as I have loved you, you also should love one another.—John 13:34

The Art of Acceptance

"ost of the unhappiness in marriage could be cured if each person would realize that you cannot change the other person but you can always change yourself." These words from a marriage counselor carry a secret to marriage happiness, for a fitting foundation for marriage is a true acceptance of each other as you are.

A happy marriage is not a lucky meeting of two meant for each other, so much as a patient, persistent path of devotion to each other in spite of failures and differences. We confess we are not perfect. It is strange that we seem so surprised when we find imperfection in the life of our partner.

Imperfection of course! But this discovery need not bring disillusionment. The wedding ceremony calls for each to accept the other as you are, "for better or for worse." The important thing in marriage is to accept, not try to change your partner. The desire to change the other person arises chiefly out of selfishness and hate rather than out of concern and love.

Some, no doubt, marry with the intention of changing the other after marriage. A wedding, however, never changes the fundamental disposition of husband and wife. Don't try the reform and refashion approach. Such strivings seldom succeed, and should they succeed, it is of doubtful improvement. The only hope is in changing one's own attitude and spirit of acceptance.

It is good to realize that certain differences will always exist. A husband and wife naturally approach problems differently.

Failure to understand basic differences can cause tension and friction. But accepting each other in love without seeking to reform the other, opens opportunities of building strong bonds. For in their differences husband and wife complement each other. Reason without emotion is lifeless, and emotion without reason is helpless. We are not called to be alike. Rather, we are challenged to contribute what the other lacks.

This does not resign us to run in a rut or make feeble and fruitless excuses such as "I am the way I am." Instead, it challenges us to become together what God would have us become. It is a call and a challenge to cultivate the characteristic you admire.

Paul L. Howe in *Sex and Religion Today* writes: "Much marriage difficulty and unhappiness are due to the failure of the partners to accept the fact of their finiteness and its meaning. Instead, they hold themselves up to ideals of performance possible only to God."

I like the little boy's definition of a friend: "someone who knows all about you and likes you just the same." So also a true lover is one who knows all about you and loves you more and more.

Marriage involves seeing and understanding the other person as he really is and loving him just that way. Our first obligation is to make the other happy, not good.

It is only by love that we lift another. Love can bring out qualities that otherwise would remain hidden.

PRAYER

Teach us, our Father, to accept each other fully and to show our love in doing the daily, humble tasks with radiance. Help us to love and serve in such a way that any personal sacrifice may seem small and every opportunity to serve may be done with joy. Amen.

Blessed is that marriage
Where satisfaction is not sought
In things or wealth,
But in larger stores of kindness and companionship.

Such shall treasure
Graces greater than gold
And reap rich rewards
Which shall remain
When gold and glitter are gone.

Then the Lord God said, "It is not good that the man should be alone; I will make him a helper as his partner."—Genesis 2:18

Considerate Companions

ven though two persons live in the same house and eat daily at the same table, it is possible to experience great loneliness. Strange as it may sound, lovers need to cultivate continued companionship in marriage, just as they did in courtship. William E. Hulme writes, "Infidelity usually begins in companionship." Dullness soon develops in the best of marriages if lovers do not learn to share intimately their plans, pleasures, hopes, wishes, work, and affection.

To be considerate companions therefore means participating in the personality of the one who belongs to the other in a total and exclusive way. Marriage calls for sharing on the physical, psychological, intellectual, social, and spiritual levels. There is more truth than exegetical accuracy in the observation of the old interpreters who said that woman was not taken from the head of man to rule over him, or from the foot to be his slave, but from his side to symbolize that she is his companion in all of life.

Thus the life of lovers is not all passion and ecstasy but consideration for one another as companions in all the duties and delights of life. Doing daily duties for and with one another drives out drudgery and deepens devotion. The least significant act can become a labor of love. The humdrum is hallowed when it is not just a matter of fulfilling functions but the formation of a flourishing fellowship.

Sex, parenthood, or work will not sustain marriage alone. Some couples who have failed to cultivate close companionship have found their marriage become empty when the children were grown or after retirement. To be meaningful, marriage must be companionship in the common and complex daily experience. The old saying that joys are doubled and sorrows are divided when shared with the one you love is true.

Companionship then is based on common interests shared. Nothing enriches and encourages companionship more than the expression of mutual appreciation. On the other hand, there is no faster train to destruction than disparaging remarks and carping criticism. Criticism pollutes the atmosphere, poisons the mind, and sets the stage for separation and heartache. Consideration avoids faultfinding and snap judgments. It will deplore hot words and cold silences.

A woman who expresses pride in her husband's work gives him greater stature and stability. Usually, the quality of a man's work is a reflection of his wife's inspiration. A wife can be her best and look her loveliest when she knows she is appreciated for the little things of life. And appreciation is expressed in such statements as: "How lovely you look," "How well you spoke," "It was a good supper," and "The house looks beautiful."

As a critical mood grows until it becomes unendurable, so a sense of gratitude grows into a deepening companionship and enjoyment.

Some psychologists say rather strongly that there are no two completely compatible people. At least we are not born compatible. This means that we must be considerate. It means that if we are to have a happy companionship we must continue to revamp our lives out of love for each other.

Improvement always involves some change in little or large

things. If there is to be a growing companionship in marriage, we must continually consider what can and needs to be changed to bring us into a closer oneness. Otherwise there is trouble.

In the play *The Odd Couple*, two men who are unable to live with their wives decide to live with one another. Each brings along the same habits, quirks, and character he brought originally to his marriage. When the curtain falls, the men are separating for the same reasons they left their wives. Neither was willing to change himself to make a go of companionship.

Remember that even though we may have great differences, there can be a close companionship if we practice consideration.

PRAYER

O God, create within us a greater capacity for companionship. Free us, our Father, from all pretense and pettiness. Deliver us from desires which drive us from you and from one another. May we cherish all that calls us into closer companionship. Make us poor in persisting in our own way and rich in real love in every relationship. Amen.

Blessed is that marriage
Which takes the long look
And knows the sweetness
Of anticipation,
Which decides not only
For one day
But for decades
And for beyond death.

Such shall know proper restraint
In each choice,
And clear vision
When expediency presses.
Such shall know the blessed bond
Of building together
Through time and eternity.

Wisdom is a fountain of life to one who has it.
—*Proverbs 16:22*

Adjustments Abundant

o move from singleness to marriage takes only a few minutes. To adjust one's habits and outlook to being married takes the rest of life.

Perhaps the most crucial time for a marriage is the first few years. This is the period of major adjustments. A large proportion of marriages that end in divorce come to grief during the first five years. Some people have called the first year of married life "the period of disillusionment." It is probably better to call it "the period of adjustment."

No two people are exactly alike. We are distinct individuals with personal patterns of feeling, behavior, and thought. Environments and backgrounds are different. There are different likes and dislikes. This is good. People would be boring if all were alike, if all came from similar backgrounds, and if all reacted alike.

But while such variety produces interest and is desirable, it also produces problems. Some people are so anxious for marital success that they will not admit problems such as every marriage faces. For this they suffer. Yet suffering in silence is seldom a solution.

What can be done?

First, we must face problems frankly and recognize differences as a normal part of life. This is a sign of maturity. So we will find happiness in marriage more quickly by unselfishly facing differences together than by striving to live in a dream world.

Discuss differences. You may not always see alike. But even difficulties can be delightful if you face them together.

Adjustment takes time. It remains a lifelong challenge. Do not think it failure if adjustment in many areas takes years to accomplish. According to studies, only about half of married couples are well adjusted from the beginning in money matters. About half experience mutual sex satisfaction from the beginning; for ten percent, it takes twenty years or more. The question in making adjustments is not Who is right? or What is right? but How can we improve together?

In marriage certain graces of character and disposition are discovered for the first time. Also some faults, peculiarities of habit, taste, and temper are faced for the first time. Many things may look alike in the moonlight, but they are different in the daylight. Here is the challenge of blending two lives into one noble, stronger, fuller, deeper, and richer life.

Facing issues frankly means to talk over differences of all kinds no matter how large or small. This does not mean that we make our marriage a debating society. But we do not understand the other's point of view until we take time to talk and listen. Talking together about minor or major concerns is a mark of maturity.

Be willing to compromise. Many things which cause difficulty are really nonessentials to happiness. One way of doing a certain thing is as good as another. If it becomes a fifty-fifty proposition, little is lost while much may be gained.

Cultivate a sense of humor. Happy is the home in which members can laugh off little happenings or mistakes which, if allowed to linger, can cause irritation. Develop the funny bone instead of the tear ducts. Thackeray wrote, "A good laugh is sunshine in a house." The Scripture says, "A merry heart doeth

good like a medicine." If we insist on weeping when our ways
are crossed, we will eventually weep alone.

With hope to quiet the coming of each dawn,
And faith that never dies,
Give me the gift of laughter, oh, I pray—
Laughter instead of sighs.
—*Elizabeth Davis Richards*

Finally, find areas of agreement. Such areas should and can
be strengthened. In most marriages there is basic agreement on
major questions. It is the small daily decisions which cause dispute.
Back of surface disagreement lies a deeper oneness if it is
sought in love and patience.

Thus, marriage is a test for strong souls. It opens greater
opportunities for growth than any other relationship in life.

PRAYER

Our Father, we thank you that your aid is always available.
In the strains that are sure to come, never let us forget the
persistence and preciousness of patience, the timelessness
and treasure of truth, and the lifting and lasting character
of love. Amen.

FORMULA FOR A HAPPY HOME

Never both be angry at once.
Never taunt the other with a past mistake.
Never forget the happy hours of early love.
Never meet without a loving welcome.
Never talk at each other, either alone or in a crowd.
Never yell at each other unless the house is on fire.
Let each one strive oftenest to yield to the other's wishes.
Let self-denial be the daily aim and practice of each.
Never let the sun go down on any anger or grievance.
Never allow a reasonable request to have to be made twice.
Never make a public remark at the expense of the other. It may seem funny sometimes, but it hurts.
Never sigh for what might have been, but make the best of what is.
Never find fault unless it is certain that a fault has been committed. Even then, always speak lovingly.
Never part for the day without a loving word to think about during the absence. Short words in the morning make a long day.
Never forget that the nearest approach to heaven on earth is where two souls rival each other in unselfishness.
Never let any fault that you have committed go by until you have confessed it and been forgiven.
Never be content until you know that both of you are walking the straight and narrow road, each helping the other.

Author Unknown

Be kind to one another, tenderhearted, forgiving one another, as God in Christ has forgiven you.—Ephesians 4:32

Forgetting what lies behind.—Philippians 3:13

Forgive and Forget

ne husband said, "While we were talking my wife got historical." "You mean hysterical," his friend corrected. "No, I mean historical," the man replied. "She brought up everything I had ever done."

Learn to forgive freely. Robert Louis Stevenson said, "To marry is to domesticate the recording angel."

At your wedding you accepted each other for what you are, not for what you were or with reservations as to what you shall yet learn about each other. Since none of us live perfect lives, we all need forgiveness. "Forgive us our debts, as we forgive our debtors" has implications first for husband and wife.

The poet Cowper wrote, "The kindest and the happiest pair will find occasion to forbear; and something, every day they live, to pity and perhaps forgive."

"Forgive me" is a phrase which should find frequent use in every family. It should of course be said sincerely.

For still in mutual sufferance lies
The secret of true living.

Love scarce is love that never knows
The sweetness of forgiving.

"The whole fellowship of marriage is ultimately based on forgiveness," David R. Mace writes in *Whom God Hath Joined* (The Westminster Press, 1953). "Two people unable to forgive cannot endure to live together as a married couple. That is why the courts of law are so clumsy and so helpless in dealing with marriage problems. The law is concerned with offense and retribution, with the neatly balanced justice that makes the punishment fit the crime. . . . But so long as marriage remains in any sense a relationship, it must be conducted upon an entirely different principle—the principle of repentance and forgiveness."

A second step is a readiness to forget. A good memory of mistakes in marriage is a vice which creates heavy and crippling burdens. There is no hope for happiness in harboring hurt feelings or thoughts. In marriage of all places, we cannot live in the past.

Yet it is at this point of recalling past mistakes that many marriages make shipwreck. Why do we mention the mistakes of others? Because we refuse to face some failure we have made. Because we attempt to justify or escape our error by a childlike pointing the finger at another.

We must, if we are to be happy together, learn the discipline of forgiving and forgetting.

"Forgetting what lies behind," we press on. In marriage we cannot allow ourselves to be chained to yesterday's mistake or last year's failure. Bygones must be bygones. It is only a misguided sense of loyalty which points to past mistakes. Bridges must be burned, and with God's help they can be.

The little words, "I remember what you did," and "I remember what you said," can only hurt. They never help. Spurgeon says it beautifully: "Love stands in the presence of a fault with a finger on her lips."

PRAYER

Our Father, it is so difficult to forget another's mistake and so easy to point the finger, to remind the other of failing and faults. Help us to forgive as Christ forgives and to forget another's failures as you forget our failures, so that we may help one another to grow in your likeness. Amen.

3

Devoted to Worthy Objectives

True love's the gift which God has given
To man alone beneath the heaven;
It is not fantasy's hot fire,
Whose wishes, soon as granted, fly;
It liveth not in fierce desire,
With dead desire it doth not die;
It is the secret sympathy,
The silver link, the silken tie,
Which heart to heart and mind to mind
In body and in soul can bind.
   —*Sir Walter Scott in*
   The Lady of the Lake

HAPPINESS AHEAD

Happy homes do not depend on expensive paintings on the wall or exquisite carpets on the floor. Carpets and comforts do not constitute happiness. Happiness is found only when it is given away. There is no place in all creation which provides so many opportunities to give and experience happiness as in marriage.

Three things are too wonderful for me;
  four I do not understand:
the way of an eagle in the sky,
  the way of a snake on a rock,
the way of a ship on the high seas,
  and the way of a man with a girl.—Proverbs 30:18-19

Different from Dreams

s it possible that I misjudged my husband that much?" These words from a wife of a few days might well describe the thoughts of every married person at some time or other. In marriage, we not only get the attractive aspects of our spouse; we get the hidden warts too.

In marriage we must modify the marital role which our expectations held before marriage. Not in the sense that now we are doomed to something less grand than expected so much as now we must face the fact that marriage is not a continual state of heavenly bliss. It is for better or for worse. And we know ourselves well enough to realize we do not always reach our highest hopes. Let us not expect perfection in our partner.

There are graces of character and disposition discovered for the first time. There are also faults, peculiarities of habit, taste, and temper never suspected, which are now seen clearly. Do not be discouraged. Here is where love plays its noblest part in blending two lives in one stronger, fuller, deeper, and richer life.

Put it down, there has never been a perfect marriage. There are many happy marriages, but probably no completely compatible marriage.

Alexander Pope wrote: "They dream in courtship, but in wedlock wake." When we wake up bewildered by the early problems of marriage, we may wonder what is happening to our marriage. We find even loving husbands and wives can be rude and crude. For marriages are made of real men and women. Each individual has fears, faults, and failings.

In marriage we must be realistic. No one marries the perfect person dreamed about. The first failure, whatever it may be, is bound to bring bitter disappointment. And here, in the early days, marriage meets real testing. How a couple decides to deal with disappointments is a central crisis of that marriage. Now is the time to learn to love deeply the other for what the person is and not for the masterpiece we hoped would be.

H. G. Wells wrote what is likely true of every husband and wife: "A day arrives in every marriage when the lovers must face each other, disillusioned, stripped of the last shred of excitement—undisguisedly themselves." While previously we saw only the best, now also we see each other at our worst. Such times can be awfully unromantic. Such times can also be the start of real romance.

Few, if any, find all they had hoped for. Since no one is perfect, marriage is a time to press toward perfection. It is important to hold the highest ideals for our marriage while remembering we are imperfect persons with possibilities of gradually growing into every good grace. It is important therefore to see each other as we are and also as we may become.

The closer the union and the higher the hopes, the greater will be the sense of disappointment at failure. Not understanding this truth can cause deepest disappointment, which if not faced frankly, can bring great loneliness.

In courtship, love stresses similarities rather than differences. In marriage, because of its constant closeness, differences become more dramatic. This is the time to put love into practice. A good motto for marriage partners is the familiar one: "God, grant me the serenity to accept the things I cannot change, the courage to change the things I can, and true wisdom to know the difference."

PRAYER

Our Father, we praise you for the promise of your presence always. You know all things. Fortify us for the unexpected and give us faith for the unexplained. Amid the things which change, keep clear and dear to us the things which remain. Free us from every chain forged by the failure of our human nature, so that we may better do your bidding. Amen.

*Blessed is that marriage
Which continues to believe
That faults will be corrected
And that the present problems,
Which press so persistently today,
Will pass away.*

*For such, each new sunrise
Speaks of new opportunity
And each hour
Holds new prospect for good.*

But the wisdom from above is first pure, then peaceable, gentle, willing to yield, full of mercy and good fruits, without a trace of partiality or hypocrisy.—James 3:17

Love is patient; love is kind.—1 Corinthians 13:4

Dealing with Differences

In every marriage there are many differences between husband and wife. This is true not only because of varied habits and ways of thinking but also because each is born with different traits, reared in different homes, and molded by different influences. In addition, one is male and the other female.

To find differences in each other is not strange and does not mean the other's way is inferior. Personal ways of doing things and dislikes and likes in such areas as diet and dress, music and manners are largely learned.

In marriage, such differences can add dimension if we determine to learn together. Differences also add beauty, even as the beauty of the rainbow becomes possible only because of many different colors.

How do we deal with differences? First, face the fact that they exist. Many articles appear in magazines on how to get along in marriage. Some suggest steps or secrets to success. Others list ten rules which are guaranteed to work. Though there may be disagreement as to how to succeed, all agree that there will be differences and quarrels at times. Couples who boast, "We've never quarreled," probably have a good forgetter (which is fine to have) or have never frankly faced differences (which is not good).

"Some of the differences in marriage come . . . from the fact that the opposite sex so readily becomes the opposition sex," George E. Sweazey writes (*In Holy Marriage*, Harper & Row, New York, 1966). "Men and women see things from different points of view, and it takes two points of view to give a depth perception."

Second, realize that each marriage is unique. Don't imagine we can make our marriage like some other. It is unfair, really impossible. Such attempts can end up only in comparing the desirable factors of another's marriage with the undesirable factors of our own. Thus, to desire the design of some other marriage is not only delightful daydreaming; it is also damaging.

In one home, the wife mows the lawn and takes care of servicing the car. In another, this would not work. We do not deal with differences by making comparisons, but by complete frankness on what works best for us.

Your marriage partner is also unique. Don't set out to change the other person. If you want someone like your father or mother, then you still need a parent rather than a husband or wife. So never allow yourself to compare your husband to your father or your wife to your mother. The happiest mate is not the one who married the best person, but the one who makes the best of the one he married. Too often we say, "If he or she were only different!" More important is the question, "What if I were different?"

A step toward a permanent and satisfying marriage may be disillusionment—that is, the willingness to accept one's self and one's partner for better or for worse on the level of everyday living.

We dreamed for a long time that married life was something out of this world. But we find our feet are still on the same old earth. Does this mean something has gone wrong? Of course not! Marriage is not so much a state as a process of becoming together. We cannot persist in pursuing the pattern of the past.

Third, happy marriages are made by the willingness of each spouse to adapt to the particular differences the other brings to marriage. This is the way to enrichment. When the major satisfaction is seeking the happiness of the other, a basic requirement for a happy marriage relationship is realized.

PRAYER

Help us, our Father, to grow together in the wisdom of love. May we sense the needs of each other and be gentle, easy to talk to, and full of mercy and good fruits which flow from genuine love. Keep us from becoming disagreeable when disappointed. Teach us how to maintain a hopeful and helpful spirit even when discouraged. Deliver us from the delusion that nothing can be bettered right where we are. Amen.

Blessed is that marriage
Where no blame is cast
During times of misfortune,
Where the spirit is one of sympathy
And the desire is to understand.

Such shall be like a stream
Fresh and overflowing
Which makes music
As it runs against the rocks
And becomes purer
By passing through obstructions.

Be sure that no one repays a bad turn by a bad turn; good should be your objective always, among yourselves and in the world at large.—1 Thessalonians 5:15, J. B. Phillips translation

Problems Produce Progress

Read Romans 12:17-21

emember," the veteran preacher said to the happy pair just married, "marriage is wonderful, but it does not solve any of your problems." It's not supposed to. Two people combine their problems when they marry. That's why marriage is for mature persons. The same situations which may end in divorce for some provide maturity and better understanding for others.

We always expected to get married someday. We dreamed about it. But likely we didn't dream about misunderstandings, financial problems, blackened food in the oven, dirty dishes stacked high in the sink, and mountains of clothes to be washed and ironed.

Yes, marriage is the highest, holiest, and happiest of human relationships. It is also the most difficult. The road two lovers travel together has the rough and rugged as well as the romantic and rosy.

"It is not destiny that makes a person the one true love; it is life," George E. Sweazey writes (*In Holy Marriage*, Harper & Row, New York, 1966). "It is hardships that have been faced together. It is the bending over children's sickbeds and struggling over budgets; it is a thousand good-night kisses and good-morning smiles; it is the vacations at the seashore and conversation in the dark; it is a growing reverence for each other which comes out of esteem and love."

Problems can produce progress in marriage. It is the difficulties more than the delights which add dimension to marriage. And a willingness to meet difficulties together is a good sign of growing maturity. Our lives are strengthened together by struggle, by common cooperation, and by reaching with joined hands after greater good.

That thorny path, those stormy skies,
Have drawn our spirits nearer;
And rendered us, by sorrow's ties,
Each to the other dearer.

Love, born in hours of joy and mirth,
With mirth and joy may perish;
That to which darker hours gave birth.
Still more and more we cherish.
    —Bernard Barton

Making promises at the marriage altar is a great act and a high point. It is surpassed only when you reaffirm it; when you face failure and your spouse says, "It doesn't matter. I married you for richer, for poorer, for better, for worse, and I know it will be better"; when you whisper to your wife in a hospital room, "I will always love you in sickness and in health."

Yes, every marriage faces difficulties and problems. And each partner accepts the problems as well as the privileges of marriage. The important thing is to discuss difficulties; don't give up because of an occasional storm. Rather, continue to both face the same direction.

Remember, when problems come it is not time to throw up our hands and say, "It's the end." Rather, it is time to roll up our sleeves and say, "This is the beginning," the beginning to building greater oneness. Phillips Brooks saw it this way: "There are ten ways of putting out a fire, but running away is not one of them."

The road is not always on the brow of the hill overlooking beauty below. Sometimes the road of life winds through the monotonous dusty valleys. But the highest hilltops are never attained except by those who willingly walk together with consecrated footsteps the weary way of the valley.

PRAYER

O God, our Father, we thank you for sunshine and shadows. Help us somehow to see the good and growth which storm clouds bring. May we understand that refreshing showers do not fall from clear skies and that trouble can turn into good to those who love you and into growth to those who look to you. Amen.

Blessed is that marriage
Which learns early the art
Of dividing care
And multiplying joy
By sharing them together.

Such shall know
That the burdens of life
Are never too heavy to bear
And that the joys of life
Are always there to share.

Bear one another's burdens, and in this way you will fulfill the law of Christ.—Galatians 6:2

Trying for Togetherness

Every marriage counselor hears the sad stories of husbands who spend all their leisure time in taverns, or at clubs, or with male cronies in some sport or favorite spot. Similar stories are told by husbands whose wives have so many interests and hobbies outside the home that their spouse seldom sees them, except when it can hardly be avoided. It is possible to live in the same house, yet in a different world.

Marriage takes togetherness to succeed. "We" comes before "I" in the word "wedding." And in the wedding ceremony the word is "we" not "I." The most dangerous day of marriage is not during the fourth, fifth, or fiftieth year. It's the day when lovers stop playing, planning, and pulling together.

During courtship and when first married, couples cannot see enough of each other. Instinctively their love inspires them with the desire to be together. Their love leads them to do things together.

One of the pitfalls after marriage is that each becomes busy in private pursuits and, if particular care is not taken, life is lived so that a spirit of togetherness is largely lost. The

Scripture says we fulfill the law of love by sharing each other's concerns, by bearing each other's burdens, and by caring so much for each other that a unity of dependence and devotion develops.

Usually, the husband is the biggest threat to togetherness. He may get wrapped up in business. He may come home tired. The wife who can be starved for companionship by the time he walks in after work may feel something has happened to their love.

At this point, however, a wife can drive a wedge between her husband and herself. If she allows pity to get hold of her, she may begin to nag her husband. Instead of speaking to him about his work and sharing his concerns, she accuses him of always working or being away too much. She may resent and resist her husband rather than restore his strength and cooperate with him. Thus she may drive him away still more to escape her complaints.

A wife is a great source of encouragement to her husband when she instills in him the feeling that in whatever he is doing she is "with him." A husband is a great source of strength to his wife when he supports her with approval and admiration and when he often takes time to spend special moments with her.

What is togetherness then? It is love taking time for each other, talking quietly together, or walking in the woods. Togetherness is taking time to speak tender words and to do extra favors.

As in courtship the happiest moments were those when we were with one another, so marriage is made happy by being together and doing many things together.

Togetherness does not just happen. It takes conscious effort. Those who would build togetherness must consciously plan things together and constantly share life together. It will mean not only making the moments of each day together meaningful but also seeking out special times for togetherness.

A growing sense of belonging to each other is also achieved by working together for others, rather than focusing all attention on oneself. As one writer says, "Life has taught us that love does not consist in gazing at each other, but in looking outward together in the same direction."

PRAYER

O Guardian of our way, travel with us always. Give to us not only a safe journey but a satisfying journey. As we begin, bind your loving care about us. May we never become too busy to stop by the babbling brook or within the shadow of some lofty peak to see your work and not ours alone. Teach us to take time for togetherness—with one another and with thee. Amen.

AT NIGHTFALL

I need so much the quiet of your love,
   After the day's loud strife;
I need your calm all other things above,
   After the stress of life.

I crave the haven that in your
      heart lies,
   After all toil is done;
I need the starshine of your heavenly
      eyes,
   After the day's great Sun.
   —Charles Hanson Towne*

*From Sunrise to Starlight by May Detherage, Abingdon Press, Nashville, Tenn., 1966.

Therefore a man leaves his father and his mother and clings to his wife, and they become one flesh.—Genesis 2:24

Romance and Relatives

The ardent young man who told his wife-to-be, "I'm marrying you; I'm not marrying your family," was no doubt speaking his adoration. He was also showing his immaturity. In a real sense we take our relatives with us. And we can choose to take a dim view of in-laws or to delight in those who are nearest to the one we love. Good in-law relationships go hand in hand with a happy home.

Marriage makes us a part of a new family. Several simple observations may help here. First, do not overlook the debt we owe to our in-laws. We have each other because of them. Our gratitude and love should reach out to them in every way possible. In spite of all the stories of difficulties with in-laws, most experience good relationships. Parents who have loved since birth cannot be expected to suddenly drop all concern. Value their interest. From now on we belong to three families: the husband's family, the wife's family, and our own new family.

Rather than look upon in-laws as stereotypes, consider them as people, as human beings having good points as well as weak points. Allow them the same freedom in having faults as we desire them to allow us.

Second, marriage means that the relationship to parents is greatly changed. Our home is a new creation. We should not try to make it a copy of the home from which we came. The focal point of our love and concern is changed. Our new home, not our parental home, is now the point of affection. There comes a time, says the writer of Genesis, when we have to leave.

Some can travel far but carry the image of father and mother along. In marriage, our partner now comes in love and importance before father and mother. Devotion is to each other above parents.

This does not mean that we cease to be a son and a daughter. Nor do we cease to love, honor, and respect our parents. It certainly does not mean that father and mother can or should be ignored or completely excused from our lives. Rather, it means that our first loyalty, under all circumstances, is to each other. Marriage requires a restructuring of love and loyalties.

At marriage the parents must realize that the purpose of parenthood has ended. Sometimes it is difficult for parents or young people to let go. But marriage means that we settle our own problems as husband and wife, and this can be a most blessed and building experience.

In ancient times, parents presented a dowry to their daughter when she married. The express purpose of this dowry was that the young married couple might have sufficient resources to set up a home of their own.

It is usually a sad day when a couple lives under the parents' roof. The old proverb, "No house is big enough for two families," refers particularly to the problem of married children living with or in the same house as parents. The Scripture in speaking of leaving and cleaving seems to refer to such complications. Every marriage has a right to its own home.

A few final notes should be added. Do not compare your married partner with your parents. The little words, "My father said," or "My mother did it this way," are shortcuts to discord, misery, and tragedy. Accept each other as you are and do not crave copies of your parents in anything.

Never use in-laws as weapons. "You're just like your mother," is an angry phrase sometimes used in quarreling. It is a loaded expression and is destructive.

Real joy and happiness result from proper attitudes toward parents. When parents can say, "We have not lost a daughter; we have gained a son," and when the newly married can sincerely say, "We feel that we have now two mothers and two fathers," bonds are built and barriers are broken. Such attitudes turn in-laws into "in-loves."

PRAYER

Heavenly Father, today we thank you for those who gave us birth and contributed so much to the building of our lives. Guide us in every relationship to show proper respect and love for our parents. Help us to learn the lesson of first loyalties as now we have covenanted our love to each other first and forever. Amen.

Blessed is that marriage
Which does not long
For larger lands
At cost of greater goals,
Which envies not
A neighbor's wealth
Or spends beyond its own.

Such shall not dread
To meet each month
Because of bills unpaid,
But rather know
A deep content
Which rather binds and builds.

Give me neither poverty nor riches;
feed me with the food that I need,
or I shall be full, and deny you,
and say, "Who is the Lord?"
or I shall be poor, and steal,
and profane the name of my God.—Proverbs 30:8-9

Facing Finances

Read Matthew 6:24-34

olomon's prayer shows keen understanding of human nature. It is not natural to pray such a prayer. We sometimes think wealth would solve everything. But external factors are not the foundation for happiness. Too much or too little can create problems. However, in present-day living the income is not the problem as much as mismanagement.

In all research done thus far, there is little correlation between the amount of money people have and their happiness in marriage. The quality of marital happiness is not related to the size of income. A Gallup Poll found that both rich and poor believe a 10 percent increase in income would solve their financial worries.

So it is not the amount of money so much, but the attitude which brings either safety or struggle. Common virtues, such as faith, self-control, honesty, and integrity, have more to do with the making of a happy home than money.

Still, money is important. Money and things are both necessary and normal. And a married couple may find that finances are a big factor which can bring them closer together or drive them apart. Through the use of money, husband and wife can evidence their love or selfishness. The use of money can provide limitless and daily opportunities to manifest love through sacrifice for each other.

Families do not begin on the basis of difference but on the basis of affection. Yet it happens many times after marriage that money and things take precedence over common concern for each other. Materialistic concerns such as a fine house, a good income, comfort, or security can wrench marital harmony and bring headache and hardship. Be assured at the start that happiness does not necessarily increase by moving to a more expensive house or earning a higher salary.

Overindebtedness is the most common financial difficulty for couples. Problems arise because of "easy credit." People who have unmet emotional needs seem to be more likely to use credit to buy things they can't afford.

Unrealistic standards in relation to income are particularly dangerous. Moonlighting on the part of the husband or wife often compounds problems rather than solving them.

A particular problem for many newlyweds is the desire for instant gratification. Social pressures may push a young couple into overindebtedness to buy a car, a home, expensive furnishings, or sports equipment.

Studies suggest that people who are insecure seek security and acceptance by buying new and expensive things, thus running themselves into debt and marriage difficulty.

So the selfish search for money can cause the loss of many things money cannot buy. Money cannot buy love. It is no substitute for tender affection. It cannot bring trustworthiness or fidelity. Happy the husband and wife who learn to share poverty or prosperity together with gratitude.

Yes, the prayer of King Solomon is a good one to pray: May God grant neither too little nor too much. May he give what he knows is best. And may he always be recognized as Giver and Lord of all things.

PRAYER

Our Father, we thank you for material blessings. Do not allow the dust of the world's desire to blur or blind our eyes. Help us see your guiding stars and the value of things invisible and eternal. Deliver us daily from the pitiful poverty which puts primary trust in the passing and forgets those things which outlast time. You know all the way ahead. Give us not only light for the way but the kind of commitment which follows wherever the light leads. Amen.

A PLEDGE FOR HUSBAND AND WIFE

As husband and wife, we will take time for love and companionship. We will keep adding fuel to the fire of love by words and acts of appreciation for each other. When there is a misunderstanding, we will be quick to forgive and to ask forgiveness. We will allow no one to come between us.

We will take a sane attitude toward money and decide financial matters together. We will take a mature attitude toward work, each carrying a proper share of family duties.

We will take time for wholesome recreation and new experiences that are worthwhile. We will keep a sense of humor and learn to laugh even at ourselves.

We will avoid the home-wrecking habits of impatience, worry, nagging, jealousy, and all other forms of self-love. We will face all hardships with faith in God and each other.

If God entrusts children to us, we will welcome them, love them, and give them good care and training.

We will give Christ his place in our hearts and in our home, keeping in tune with him by frequent periods of Bible reading and prayer. As a family we will be loyal members of the church, attending its services together regularly and sharing in its ministry to others.

By God's help our home will be an asset and not a liability to the church, to the community, and to the world.—Ruth B. Stoltzfus*

One's life does not consist in the abundance of posses-sions.—Luke 12:15

Faithful
Stewards

Read 2 Corinthians 9

od is interested in having us know that things in themselves do not make for happiness. On the wedding day we expect to find love and happiness in each other. In marriage, then, we should not be caught in a frantic search to find satisfaction in things.

This does not mean that financial concerns are not real ones or even at times distressing ones in every marriage. It means that a true concept of Christian stewardship puts all of life in proper perspective. Money dare not be master but servant. God calls us to be faithful stewards of all we have. We dare not be careless. Further, to be good stewards requires self-denial and sacrifice on the part of both husband and wife.

In the beginning of marriage, it is good to consider carefully what is included in being good stewards. Carelessness in temporal things can cause much marriage tension. Here are some good guides which may help.

Figure out your exact income. Don't include "possibilities," or the raise you are planning on, or the bonus you might get at the end of the year.

List your expenses. Put down every running cost, such as

housing, food, clothing, car. Included here should be a regular saving plan. Set aside some savings regularly. Many young married couples simply live from one payday to the next, hoping a windfall will come and present them a key to an address on Easy Street. It seldom happens.

Include a system of regular giving. The Scriptures call the Christian to give cheerfully and regularly. In fact, keep this out first and start with a tenth of your income. This may look difficult to a young couple starting out in marriage. It has, however, an immeasurable effect on the spiritual tone and atmosphere of the home.

Work out a plan or budget together. In marriage a partnership of the purse is paramount. A steady income does not solve all the money matters in marriage. The secret is a cooperating for the good of both. Better even than a budget is the blessing of discussing items to purchase together.

An essential rule is to purchase nothing important until both husband and wife have agreed upon it. Avoid impulse buying. Usually, something that cannot wait to be bought until tomorrow is not worth purchasing today. List the things you don't need at present but which you want to work toward in the future.

As Christian stewards, avoid the pressure of installment buying. Piling up bills means plenty of trouble. A person of good, honest character does not demand luxuries he can't afford. To do so often means the difference between harmony and heartache.

Finally, don't expect to start where your parents are now. Recent studies indicate that young married couples assume marriage will immediately bring with it most of the equipment that it took their parents years to acquire. Some feel that furniture must be as new as their marriage. But it is best not to blow savings to buy things.

Taste takes time to jell. Some interior decorators go so far as to say that young couples should avoid buying anything expensive in the first four or five years. Experiment and explore before the expense.

The happiest times in many marriages are often those times which demand pulling together to make a go financially. And "better a dinner of herbs where love is than a stalled ox and hate therewith."

PRAYER

Our Father, recognizing that every blessing comes from you, help us to handle the things in our hands, the temporal, with such lightness of touch that they will always be in proper perspective to things eternal. Give us a true sense of values. May we properly discern and delight in the passing and the permanent. Amen.

Blessed is that marriage
Which, bound by inner ties,
Finds hearts united
When distance separates.

Such shall never be lonely
Even though alone.
And such shall leave home strong
To meet the world,
Yet always with the desire
To return again soon
For strength and courage.

By wisdom a house is built,
   and by understanding it is established.
      —Proverbs 24:3

There is a time for everything . . .a time to be silent and a
time to speak.—Ecclesiastes 3:1, 7, NIV

Constant Communication

ne marriage counselor was asked, "What is the most essential characteristic of a happy marriage?" He replied, "After love, being able to confide fully, freely, and frankly in each other."

Communication can be called the core of any successful marriage. When we fail to listen to each other and to talk to each other, there is deep trouble ahead. So put a premium on communication. This means to overcome the desire to conceal feelings and thoughts and then rise to the honesty of sharing joys and disappointments, and discussing wishes and misunderstandings.

When two people marry, each has an idyllic picture of what marriage should be. Many of the problems are the clashing of these pictures. Harmony and unity can come only by talking in frank and honest terms.

Sticks and stones are hard on bones.
Aimed with angry art,
Words can sting like anything.
But silence breaks the heart.—Phillis McGinley

Remember, love can survive large problems in the open better than small ones buried and smoldering within. It is the deep freeze of silence which is dangerous.

The happiest marriages are those in which both spouses are brave and honest enough to share their innermost thoughts. And the ability to talk things over without the explosions of quarreling is the mark of a growing and maturing marriage.

Solutions for most situations can be found in a short time by a clear, collected, and calm approach. Difficulties in discussion arise when the tongue is used more than the head. Sulkiness is an emotional poison sapping the very strength of marriage. One of the cruelest things is to simply ignore or refuse to talk to one's companion.

Thinking together is more important than thinking alike. And talking together about touchy problems indicates true love for each other. Communication puts love into practice.

Communication is an art. It must be learned. It doesn't just happen. It can be hindered by timidity, bashfulness, or fear of what the other will think, say, or do in reply.

Communication demands mutual trust. To share inmost thoughts, feelings, and experiences depends on the safety one feels in receiving and giving confidences, on the knowledge that what is shared will not be ridiculed or misunderstood, and on the persuasion that what is said will be taken seriously.

There is a striking statement in Scripture which says, "Do not let the sun go down while you are still angry, and do not give the devil a foothold" (Ephesians 4:26, NIV). Never go to bed angry. Although the discussion of the deep and real problems which every home has is hard, it is the best medicine for making a strong marriage.

To communicate means to forget ourselves, to listen and try to understand the other's point of view. Learn to talk together about all kinds of things. Hearts are drawn together by talking about common concerns, souls by speaking of heavenly things. Love leads to sharing because it will not deny its love.

To communicate means to rise to the level of honesty about money, fears, wishes, motivations, and sexual feelings and responses, as well as about mistakes, resentments, and misunderstandings.

Marriage dare have no room for reservations. Keep hearts open to each other. Share thoughts freely. Give bodies completely and release souls reverently to each other.

The wedlock of minds will be greater than that of bodies.—Erasmus

PRAYER

Our Father, as we have opened our hearts to you, so we also pray for open hearts to each other. Never leave our lives. Rather, enlarge your love in us to include all in need and narrow our lives so that all self-love, envy, and pride are shut out. Grant us, we pray, the power to speak true words from a heart of love, acceptable to you and helpful to others. Amen

Blessed is that home
Which is a haven for travelers
And a shelter from a cold climate,
Where guests love to come
And the home folks
Desire no better place.

Such a home
Shall be like a shelter in a rock
Providing safety in the storm,
And like a strong gate
It shall guard
And make glad
Those who dwell within.

Whatever is true, whatever is honorable, whatever is just, whatever is pure, whatever is pleasing, whatever is commendable, if there is any excellence and if there is anything worthy of praise, think about these things.
—Philippians 4:8

Seven Great and Good Guides

n somewhat summary style, the wedding service catches up great biblical ideals. Although there are variations in the marriage formula, most weddings include the following seven points in some form.

Cherish a mutual esteem and love. To cherish means to hold dear and precious. It is daily tender care. True love makes each miserable when apart and blissful when together. Married love must have deep admiration for each other, and this admiration can grow or deepen by what we say and do. To cherish a mutual esteem means we will care about the interests of the other. It means we will appreciate the thoughts and feelings of each other. And love is the climate in which mutual esteem for one another grows.

Bear with each other's infirmities and weaknesses. This is a frank confession that neither will be perfect. We will find qualities we don't like in each other. We will bear with these weaknesses and infirmities a thousand times. To continually criticize or center our thoughts on the other's failures can only complicate and make matters worse. "A quarrelsome wife is like a constant dripping," Solomon says (Proverbs 19:13, NIV).

The same could be said of a complaining husband.

Comfort each other in sickness, trouble, and sorrow. Following our wedding my wife and I learned very quickly about the adult responsibility stated in the marriage vows. The first two months, both of us became ill for a week or more, although not at the same time. First she cared for me as I lay sick in bed. Then I cared for her. The "in sickness and in health" phrase suddenly became reality.

To comfort means to strengthen, encourage, and console. At the wedding we are very realistic. Each will need the comfort of the other.

In honesty and industry, provide for each other and for your household in temporal things. Carelessness in temporal things is a chief source of marriage difficulties. Few agree at the beginning on the spending of money, but if the attitude is right and there is a willingness to talk, any couple is well on the way to happy solutions.

Pray for and encourage each other in the things which pertain to God. In marriage we became keepers of the other's soul. Augustine pointed to the final purpose of marriage: "that the one might bring the other with him to heaven." Saint Paul wrote, "Think of it: as a wife you may be your husband's salvation; as a husband you may be your wife's salvation" (1 Corinthians 7:16, NEB).

Live together as heirs of the grace of God. God has many blessings to bestow through our marriage. We will never cease needing his grace. We will need God's grace for patience, forgiveness, and understanding. And it is God's grace which pulls through the pinch of poverty, upholds in the difficult hours, and helps both in seeking and finding forgiveness.

Forsaking all others, keep yourself only unto the other as long as you both shall live. Marriage needs this attitude and dependability to develop. To give ourselves totally to another is a great decision, but is also a decision with a great binding effect. And any thought or art which turns us from the one we love is a traitor to us. There is a glorious security in caring first for each other as long as we live.

132

PRAYER

O God, we thank you that our hearts and home can be your dwelling place. Join our lives in the complete fulfillment of your will. Teach us to think first of you and of the other in love unfailing, in faith unbending, and in devotion unending. Amen.

Anyone can build an altar; it requires a God to provide the flame. Anyone can build a house; we need the Lord for the creation of a home.—John Henry Jowett in Thirsting for the Springs

Blessed is the marriage
In which each learns early
The primacy and power
Of God's Word
And united prayer.

Such shall know
The strength and sustenance
Needed for daily struggle
And the joy and peace
Of daily faith and forgiveness.

Unless the Lord builds the house, those who build it labor in vain. Unless the Lord guards the city, the guard keeps watch in vain. It is in vain that you rise up early and go late to rest, eating the bread of anxious toil; for he gives sleep to his beloved.—Psalm 127:1-2

Worship and Wisdom

n *The Fine Art of Living Together,* the late Albert W. Beaver said he sent out a questionnaire to 750 couples whom he had married. In answer to the question: "What, in your judgment, is the greatest element making for your happiness in homelife?" the largest number replied that it was "religion lived daily in the home."

Our homes are not complete or whole without God. There cannot be inner harmony without him. In fact, says the psalmist, unless the Lord builds our homes all we do is useless. Try as we may, we cannot ourselves realize our deepest desires or find satisfying rest. We need him every moment in marriage. And it is in the moments of prayer and worship that the guiding stars shine clearest in the skies and the fabric of our faith is made strong and beautiful.

> *Before the mountains were brought forth,*
> *or ever you had formed the earth*
> *and the world,*
> *from everlasting to everlasting*
> *you are God.—Psalm 90:2*

Life is lent to us as a sacred trust. To fulfill our stewardship we begin with a recognition of God's grace and goodness. We confess that he is God. What a great satisfaction it is to be assured that the God of all ages is with us! And no problem is too trivial or too hard for him.

Do not worry about anything, but in everything by
prayer and supplication with thanksgiving let your
requests be made known to God. And the peace of God,
which surpasses all understanding, will guard your hearts and
your minds in Christ Jesus.—Philippians 4:6-7

Our lives are linked with the God of creation. When we rest in this confidence and relax in his care, we need not fear for the future. Rather, we respond in bringing all our concerns to him in prayer. This means our general concerns. We are to come in supplication. This speaks about particular problems. We are to bring our requests. Requests refer to the details of each day. And don't forget to thank him daily. Few things keep us so much aware of God and his gift as thanksgiving. Joy and peace result from praise rather than plenty.

Before they call I will answer,
  while they are yet speaking
    I will hear.
      —Isaiah 65:24

The Lord is near to all who call on him. . . .
He fulfills the desire of all who fear him. . . .
—Psalm 145:18-19

We sometimes speak as though God were far away. But he is always within speaking and hearing distance. Call on him continually.

Great peace have those who love your law;
nothing can make them stumble.—Psalm 119:165

Love for doing God's will steadies our steps in the difficult days. It is the path to peace and power in the presence of trying problems. And our outlook on life is affected by our uplook to Christ.

For here we have no lasting city, but we are looking for the city that is to come.—Hebrews 13:14

Remember, in the building of your home, the fact that heaven awaits you hereafter. Make your home here a foretaste of your heavenly home. The person who perceives clearly the difference between the passing and the permanent performs the smallest duties best.

Be faithful until death, and I will give you the crown of life.
—Revelation 2:10

God's call is not to fame or fortune or even favorable circumstances, but to faithfulness. The glory of life lies in a patient, persistent ability to keep on going. A good start is not sufficient. The crown comes at the close of the Christian career. And it is worth everything we put into it, even though it cost death itself.

A lovely prayer hangs in some homes:

Lord, make my house thine
until thine shall be mine.

PRAYER

Our heavenly Father, hallow every hour with a consciousness of your constant care and companionship. Make our home your habitation, a holy of holies, so that your name may be honored. Through Jesus Christ we pray. Amen.

For Your Further Reading

Achtemeier, Elizabeth, *The Committed Marriage.*
Westminster, Philadelphia, Pa.

Amstutz, H. Clair, *Marriage in Today's World.*
Herald Press, Scottdale, Pa.

Augsburger, A. Don, Editor, *Marriages That Work.*
Herald Press, Scottdale, Pa.

Augsburger, David, *Caring Enough to Confront.*
Herald Press, Scottdale, Pa.

_____ *Caring Enough to Forgive.*
Herald Press, Scottdale, Pa.

_____ *Cherishable: Love and Marriage.*
Herald Press, Scottdale, Pa.

Butterfield, Oliver M., *Sexual Harmony in Marriage.*
Enslow Publishing, Hillside, N.J.

Crenshaw, Theresa Larsen, *Bedside Manners.*
Pinnacle Books, New York, N.Y.

DeSanto, Charles P. and Williams, Terri Robinson, *Putting Love to Work in Marriage.* Herald Press, Scottdale, Pa.

Drescher, John M., *May Your Marriage Be a Happy One.*
Herald Press, Scottdale, Pa.

Drescher, John M., and Betty, *If We Were Starting Our Marriage Again.* Abingdon, Nashville, Tenn.

Frydenger, Tom and Adrienne, *The Blended Family.*
Zondervan, Grand Rapids, Mich.

Hulme, William F., *Building a Christian Marriage.*
Prentice Hall, Augsburg, Minn.

Mace, David R., *Success in Marriage.*
Abingdon Press, Nashville, Tenn.

Schmitt, Abraham and Dorothy, *Renewing Family Life.*
Herald Press, Scottdale, Pa.

Shedd, Charlie and Martha, *Bible Study in Deuteronomy.*
Zondervan, Grand Rapids, Mich.

Small, Dwight Harvey, *Marriage as Equal Partnership.*
Baker Books, Grand Rapids, Mich.

Wright, H. Norman, *Communication: Key to Your Marriage.*
Regal, Ventura, Calif.

ohn M. Drescher of Harrisonburg, Virginia, is married to Betty Keener. They are the parents of five grown children and grandparents of twelve.

Drescher has taught at Eastern Mennonite Seminary in Harrisonburg and was pastor of Zion Mennonite Church, Broadway, Virginia. He previously served as editor of the denominational weekly, *Gospel Herald,* and as moderator of the Mennonite Church.

Drescher is the author of 32 published books. His articles have appeared in more than 100 magazines and journals, including *Reader's Digest, Christianity Today, These Times, Catholic Digest,* and *Parents Magazine.* In addition, he has conducted many family retreats and seminars across denominational lines.

Other books Drescher has written include *If I Were Starting My Family Again*, *If We Were Starting Our Marriage Again*, *Seven Things Children Need*, and *Doing What Comes Spiritually*.